Prophetic Declaration and Breakthrough

Prayers For 2020

I Will Arise And Shine

A 21 Days Fasting and Prayers to Command the Year, Receive Direction and Provoke Uncommon Favor, Restoration, and Financial Breakthrough

DANIEL C. OKPARA

CONTENTS

FREE BONUS...

Download These 4 Powerful Books Today for FREE...

And Take Your Relationship With God to a New Level.

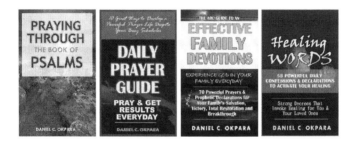

Go Here to Download:

www.betterlifeworld.org/grow

Opening Prayer

Dear Heavenly Father,

I thank You for the gift of another year.

Thank You for Your protection, preservation, and provision.

I confess that I have seen this year only by Your grace and mercy. And for that I say, thank You, Lord.

I thank You, Father, because this year is designed to bring me closer to You. It is a year that I will grow in the knowledge of Thy Word and the excellency of Your wisdom.

This year, Lord, may I walk in Your will and purpose for my life. May I seek Thy Kingdom and the manifold revelation of Thy presence every day. May my heart be drawn to Thee at all times, and may I heed the call of Thy Spirit always.

Give me the grace to walk in obedience all through this year, Lord, in Jesus name.

Father,

May all the hours, days, weeks, and months that come with this year be blessed for our families and us. May our going out be a blessing, and may our coming back be a blessing.

Preserve us continually from the arrows that fly by the day and from the pestilence that stalks at night.

O Lord, give us wisdom to always discern and escape the tricks and traps of the devil and his agents at all times this year, in Jesus name.

Amen.

Introduction

"God does not make our lives boring. He makes it more exciting than we'll ever imagine."

A few days ago, I posted the following quote on Facebook, *"It is not the best planners who succeed in life, but the most empowered..."*

By that statement, I am not trying to demean the act of planning one's life. Not at all. I am only stating an apparent reality that success in life is not a function of planning only. There is a need for empowerment as well. There is a need for spiritual enablement.

Almost every end of the year, people sit down to write what they call *New Year resolutions* or *New Year goals*. Unfortunately, statistics say that 80% fail to achieve their New Year resolutions. In fact, by February, the majority had lost the resolve for their New Year goals and resolutions and reverted to their status quo.

I agree with that finding because, for many years, I noticed that reality in my own life too. I would sit down every December and excitedly draw out beautiful plans for the upcoming year. Then I would be so full of faith in what I would do and what I would achieve. But by the next December, it would be evident that I accomplished less than 20% of what I wrote down.

It happened to me for many years until I began to ask myself questions:

- What is the best way to plan one's life each year?

- What goals should be a part of my yearly resolutions?

Then the answer hit me: *"There is a way that seems right unto a man, but it ends in death"* (Proverbs 14:12). The **death** in this scripture is not only the physical end of life. It also means failure, frustration, lack of success, and so on.

The Holy Spirit showed me that ***"unless we plan our lives with God, we are not guaranteed of success."***

This insight is what birthed the direction of coming before God every first month of the year to prayer-plan the year in God's presence. During this separation and seeking, we present the year to God, ask Him for what we should focus on for the year, speak into the year, and present our desires to Him in prayers. Since I learned to do this, I noticed that, yes, while I haven't had a 100% success rate with my yearly goals, I've had more fulfillment, more joy and happiness, more free time, and made more impact in the lives of people.

I believe that man, no matter how intelligent, is incapable of designing his path to fulfillment and happiness without God's help. This is why I teach people to come before God and plan their lives with Him.

GOD WANTS THE BEST FOR YOU

When I teach divine direction and prayer-planning your life and New Year, I often perceive people have some reservations with my view. They think that God may not lead them to accomplish big things. Fortunately, the scripture shows that God always has a better plan than ours.

In 1 Samuel 30:8, the Bible says: *"And David enquired at the Lord, saying, Shall I pursue after this troop? Shall I overtake them? And he answered him, Pursue: for thou shalt surely overtake them, and without fail recover all.*

Did you notice David's desire in this instance? He said:

- Shall I pursue the enemies?

- Shall I overcome them?

As long as he was concerned, those were the two main issues in his mind: **to pursue those enemies and kill them**.

But when God responded, He said...

- Pursue

- Overtake

- Recover all

God was not only interested in defeating the enemies. He was also interested in total restoration. Imagine if David began chasing the enemies without this revelation.

When God leads you, He leads you to aim for better and bigger things, to pursue better and bigger projects, to earn more and go for more, to live healthier and wealthier, to achieve better family union and peace.

God does not make our lives boring.
He makes it more exciting than we'll
ever imagine.

Be assured that seeking God's direction and following His plans will make your life more exciting, more fun, more challenging, and more fulfilling. Show a willingness to surrender your plans and New Year resolutions to Him and be led by Him. That's how "you shall eat the good of the land."

> "They that wait upon the Lord shall renew their strength; they shall mount up with wings as eagles; they shall run, and not be weary; and they shall walk, and not faint - Isaiah 40:31.

> "It is not of him that willeth, nor of him that runneth, but of God that sheweth mercy - Rom 9:16.

When we spend time with God and prayer-plan our New Year, we have confidence that the Spirit of God will guide our hearts to make the right decisions, empower us to follow after the right goals, and graciously achieve what truly matters.

IN THE BEGINNING, GOD...

When God is at the root of your plans and pursuits, then you are sure of success, irrespective of the challenges on the way. I have learned, at the end of the day, that God only blesses what He inspires, instructs or commands.

So instead of drawing up a bunch of lists every end of the year and chasing them every new year, come before God and say, *"Lord, guide my heart on what I must pursue in the coming year."*

Then you begin to make your plans from this level of awareness. This is the way to achieve more, earn more, and be more blessed and happy.

> 8 I will instruct you (says the Lord) and guide you along the best pathway for your life; I will advise you and watch your progress. 9 Don't be like a senseless horse or mule that has to have a bit in its mouth to keep it in line! - Psalm 32:8-9 (TLB)

How to Use This Book

This book is intended to help you spend at least 21 days in prayers, reflections, and total surrender to the LORD over the New Year. The teachings and prayers cover most aspects of life and will help you encounter God as you relate with Him and declare His Words over your life and destiny. It will help you prayer-plan your year and completely submit all to the LORD. As you do, you'll be empowered to *achieve what matters this year.*

Mary Fairchild said, *"Instead of making a New Year's resolution, consider committing to a biblical solution."*

Any way you decide to use this prayer book is up to you.

Should you decide to start praying from December 20th, January 2nd, 3rd, 10th, 20th, or even in March, August, etc. it's your entire card to play. The most important thing is that as we recognize the need to humble ourselves before God and present all to Him, He will help us move forward and enter into our promised land.

WHY FAST?

It is highly recommended that you use this book with fasting. If you go through the Bible, you'll notice that fasting is a regular practice of God's people in surrendering the flesh and seeking the LORD.

There are different kinds of fasting. However, that is not the focus of this book. Whatever type of fasting you chose to do is okay - whether it is 6 - 10 am, 6-12:00 noon, or 6 PM-6 AM – that's great.

Whether it's just skipping dinner that you decide to do, that's fine and great. What is important is that you realize the need to humble yourself before the LORD and pray.

I usually encourage people to drink water when they are fasting. If you can skip dinner to pray the prayers in this book efficiently at night, that's better. Skipping dinner fast is especially useful as it helps you to go about your business in the day and then seek the LORD for one hour or more in the nights.

As we humble ourselves before the LORD, we receive strength and direction to resist the coordinated forces of wickedness and obtain God's blessings designed for our lives.

RECOMMENDED PRAYER TIMES

While you may pray at any time, I recommend that you select any of the time sessions below:

- 12:00am – 1:00am (Midnight Session)
- 3:00 Am – 4:00 Am (Early Morning Session)
- 6:00am – 7:00am (Morning Session)
- 12:00 – 1:00pm (Midday Session)
- 3:00pm – 4:00pm (Afternoon Session)
- 9:00pm – 10:00pm (Night Session)

You may choose any of the sessions and pray for your chosen number of days. There are no mandates, which means you could chose the afternoon session today and pray and chose the midnight session tomorrow and pray. Whatever is convenient for your schedule is welcome.

More importantly, expect the power of God to move in your life.

Scripture for the Year

Isaiah 60:1-22

Meditate as you read.

₁ Arise, shine; for thy light is come, and the glory of the Lord is risen upon thee.

₂ For, behold, the darkness shall cover the earth and gross darkness the people: but the Lord shall arise upon thee, and his glory shall be seen upon thee.

₃ And the Gentiles shall come to thy light, and kings to the brightness of thy rising.

₄ Lift up thine eyes round about, and see: all they gather themselves together, they come to thee: thy sons shall come from far, and thy daughters shall be nursed at thy side.

₅ Then thou shalt see, and flow together, and thine heart shall fear, and be enlarged; because the abundance of the sea shall be converted unto thee, the forces of the Gentiles shall come unto thee.

₆ The multitude of camels shall cover thee, the dromedaries of Midian and Ephah; all they from Sheba shall come: they shall bring gold and incense, and they shall shew forth the praises of the Lord.

₇ All the flocks of Kedar shall be gathered together unto thee, the rams of Nebaioth shall minister unto thee: they shall come up with acceptance on mine altar, and I will glorify the house of my glory.

₈ Who are these that fly as a cloud, and as the doves to their windows?

₉ Surely the isles shall wait for me, and the ships of Tarshish first, to bring thy sons from far, their silver and their gold with them, unto the name of the Lord thy God, and to the Holy One of Israel, because he hath glorified thee.

₁₀ And the sons of strangers shall build up thy walls, and their kings shall minister unto thee: for in my wrath I smote thee, but in my favor have I had mercy on thee.

₁₁ Therefore thy gates shall be open continually; they shall not be shut day nor night; that men may bring unto thee the forces of the Gentiles, and that their kings may be brought.

₁₂ For the nation and kingdom that will not serve thee shall perish; yea, those nations shall be utterly wasted.

₁₃ The glory of Lebanon shall come unto thee, the fir tree, the pine tree, and the box together, to beautify the place of my sanctuary; and I will make the place of my feet glorious.

₁₄ The sons also of them that afflicted thee shall come bending unto thee; and all they that despised thee shall bow themselves down at the soles of thy feet; and they shall call thee; The city of the Lord, The Zion of the Holy One of Israel.

₁₅ Whereas thou has been forsaken and hated, so that no man went through thee, I will make thee an eternal excellency, a joy of many generations.

₁₆ Thou shalt also suck the milk of the Gentiles, and shalt suck the breast of kings: and thou shalt know that I the Lord am thy Saviour and thy Redeemer, the mighty One of Jacob.

₁₇ For brass, I will bring gold, and for iron I will bring silver, and for wood brass, and for stones iron: I will also make thy officers peace and thine exactors righteousness.

[18] Violence shall no more be heard in thy land, wasting nor destruction within thy borders; but thou shalt call thy walls Salvation, and thy gates Praise.

[19] The sun shall be no more thy light by day; neither for brightness shall the moon give light unto thee: but the Lord shall be unto thee an everlasting light, and thy God thy glory.

[20] Thy sun shall no more go down; neither shall thy moon withdraw itself: for the Lord shall be thine everlasting light, and the days of thy mourning shall be ended.

[21] Thy people also shall be all righteous: they shall inherit the land for ever, the branch of my planting, the work of my hands, that I may be glorified.

[22] A little one shall become a thousand, and a small one a strong nation: I the Lord will hasten it in his time.

Day 1: **Give Thanks**

---

*"O give thanks to the Lord, for He is good; For His lovingkindness endures forever." - **1 Chron. 16:34(AMP)***

Before we go deep into praying the revelations from our anchor scripture, we need to declare this prayer retreat open with gratitude and thanksgiving.

Being thankful isn't just for the Thanksgiving holiday. It is supposed to be a lifestyle, something we do every day. And come to think of it, we have so much to be grateful for every day.

Sometimes, the world and what we want – our many unmet needs –try to blind us from seeing a lot of what God has done and is doing. However, we must, as a matter of necessity, look away from what is not done; we must look away from our worries and begin to appreciate God from the depths of our hearts.

When praise and thanksgiving seem difficult because of the pressures of life, failures, and unanswered prayers, we should remember something called "the sacrifice of praise." This means giving thanks even when it seems like there isn't much to be thankful for. For example, Paul and Silas were thrown in jail for doing a Godly work – preaching the gospel. One would expect them to be worried about how God did not intervene to prevent that from happening. But they instead praised God. That's a sacrifice of praise.

Let's begin our New Year prayer retreat by looking deeply into our lives and coming up with gratitude and thankfulness. As we dedicate ourselves to appreciation, God's power of salvation is made manifest in our lives for the year.

PRAYER OF THANKSGIVING

"Heavenly Father,

The God of all blessings, source of all life, and giver of all grace.

I thank You for the gift of life, for the breath that sustains our lives, for the food that nourishes us, and for the love of friends and family without which we would not exist.

Thank You, Lord, for the past year, for Your protection, guidance, provision, and preservation. Thank You for the year that has come, for bringing us safely into this year, and for Your plans for us this year.

O LORD, be praised forever and ever, in Jesus name

Thank You, Lord, for the mystery of creation, for the beauty that the eye can see, for the joy that the ear can hear, for the unknown that we cannot behold, for the vastness of the universe that draws us beyond the definition of ourselves and fills us with wonders.

Thank You for setting us in communities and societies; for families who nurture our becoming; for friends who love us by choice; for companions at work, who share our daily tasks; for strangers and for people from other lands who make us wonder the depth of the world and grow in understanding.

Thank You for children who lighten our moments with delight; for the unborn, who offer us hope for the future.

O Lord, I thank You for this day, and this year, for life and for one more year to live and to work for justice and peace.

Thank You for neighbors who keep us company and teach us patience. Thank You for those who love me and those who teach and empower me to love back.

Thank You for another year to experience your presence and your promise.

For everything You have done, and all the blessings and lessons of the past, present and future, I give You thanks, through Jesus Christ, I pray.

Amen

DECLARATION OF PRAISE

(Psalm 22: 21-25)

I praise You, O Lord, for all that You have done for my family and me; You saved us from the lion's mouth, delivered us from the wild ox, and freed us from the devourer's cage.

You continue to protect and keep us safe in the world. Thank You for Your LOVE and kindness every day.

O LORD, You did not despise nor detest me when I was afflicted; neither did You hide Your face from me. I called on You severally, and You answered me and listened to me when I cried. You also helped me all through the year.

My praise will continually be of Thee O Lord. I will praise You before the world and before the congregation of Your people. And I will pay my vows made in the time of trouble, before those who reverently fear YOU.

Thank You, Everlasting Father, in Jesus name.

DECLARATION OF PRAISE

(Psalm 138:1-3)

"O LORD, our God, maker of Heaven and earth.

You are the LORD GOD ALMIGHTY.

Your praise and glory fill the earth. Your praise fills my life, and Your praise fills my family.

I thank You, Lord, with all my heart; I sing praise to You before the gods. I face Your holy Temple, bow down, and praise your name because of Your constant love and faithfulness, because You have shown that Your name and Your commands are supreme.

You answered me when I called to you; with Your strength, You strengthened me. May Your name be praised forever and ever, in Jesus name

---

O Lord, even though You are so high above, You care for the lowly, and the proud cannot hide from you.

When troubles surround me, you keep me safe. You oppose my bitter enemies and save me by your power.

You will do everything you have promised; Lord, Your love is eternal. You will complete the work that you have begun.

In Jesus name.

Day 2: **Decree and Declare**

Say unto them, 'As truly as I live, saith the Lord, as ye have spoken in mine ears, so will I do to you.' – Numbers 14:28

By the inspiration of the Holy Spirit, this year is declared the year to **Arise and Shine.** And our text is taken from Isaiah chapter 60. Read this chapter of the Bible today and personalize each verse for your life. And you will indeed arise and shine.

God's purpose for creating man is to *"let them have dominion over the fish of the sea, over the birds of the air, and the cattle, over all the earth and over every creeping thing that creeps on the earth."* And one of the methods or ways God ordained that man will achieve this purpose is through the use of his words.

Genesis 2:19 says: *"Now the LORD God had formed out of the ground all the wild animals and all the birds in the sky. He brought them to the man to see what he would name them; and whatever the man called each living creature, that was its name."*

Adam exercised his dominion over the creatures of God by declaring what they would bear, and that became their names.

> ### *Your declarations influence the outcome of life and events in and around your life.*

So let us declare God's words and promises into the year today. For "Thou shalt also decree a thing, and it shall be established unto thee: and the light shall shine upon thy ways."

DECLARATIONS

This year (.....), I will arise and shine for my light has come, and the Glory of the Lord has risen upon me. I will access every secret and knowledge required for my manifestation.

Even if darkness covers the earth and gross darkness covers the people, I will be spared, I will be safe, I will be secure, and I will always excel and shine because the

Spirit of God indwells me and God's glory is being revealed upon me and through me.

This year (.....), my manifestation will be pronounced. Nations will come to my light; kings will come to see the glory of the Lord upon me, and my testimony shall draw men and women unto the Lord.

My family shall be safe this year. My spouse and I shall grow stronger together. Our children shall be drawn to the Lord, and all they that are connected to me shall be supernaturally protected, preserved, and provided for, in Jesus name.

This year (.....), the abundance of the sea shall be converted unto me. My vision, business, and career shall receive global recognition. I shall have an abundance of health, peace, love, prosperity, and finances. I shall share wealth, money, peace, and salvation to others from the abundance of my barns.

This year (......) money shall serve me.

Scarcity shall be far from me.

When others are saying there is not enough, I shall be sharing from God's excess in my care.

Foreigners will come and build up my walls. Leaders and kings will send me support and aid, for God's mercy and grace is speaking through me this year, in the name of Jesus Christ.

This year (......), my gates will stay wide open, around the clock, to receive the wealth of many lands. And I shall not fail in my assignment as a Christian. I shall share and distribute the love of Jesus Christ to many this year.

This year (....) I shall walk in divine favor every day.

Wherever I was rejected in the past, I shall be re-accepted and doubly honored. Every respect, honor, and promotion that has eluded me in the past shall be restored to me this year.

This year, I shall be a joy to behold. People shall feel blessed knowing and working with me. Through me, lives will be made better, in Jesus name

---

All through this year (......), whatever I lay my hands to do shall prosper. For brass, God will bring gold, and for iron, God will bring silver, and for wood brass, and for stones iron.

I shall walk in integrity, and righteousness and peace shall rule over mine abode.

I will carry the presence of God in my office and company. I will excel in the work of my hands.

Throughout this year (......), there shall be no violence in my life and family. Every plan to perpetrate crime, vandalism, terrorism, violence and kidnapping around me is canceled. There'll be no more stories of crime in my land, no more robberies, and no more destruction.

This year (......), my street shall be called salvation street, and peace shall reign in our community, in Jesus name

---

This year, I shall inherit the land.

I shall reign for I am God's planting, a branch of God's hands, bringing glory to the name of Jesus.

In the name of Jesus Christ, I declare that this is my year of Manifestation. I will arise and shine for my light has come.

I shall have victory in every area of my life. I shall have victory in my family, workplace, ministry, and community.

I shall have victory in my relationship.

Whatever the devil has stolen from my life and family is getting restored 100-fold this year. My health, finances, peace, and faith is restored this year.

Nothing shall interfere with the work of the Holy Spirit being accomplished in my life.

Henceforth, no weapon fashioned against me shall prosper, and every tongue that rises against me this year shall be condemned in Jesus name.

This year, I decree that I am filled with power according to the order of Moses, Jesus, and the apostles.

I am a candidate for signs, wonders, and miracles.

I will lay my hands on the sick, and they shall recover. I shall cast out devils, and even if I drink any deadly thing by mistake, it shall not hurt me, in Jesus name.

I decree that I am free from every form of ancestral curses and problems coming from my lineage.

I declare that there is no more room for any ancestral bondage in my life and family henceforth.

May all open doors through which curses come and operate in my lineage be closed this day, in the Name of Jesus Christ.

I confess and believe that this year is my year to arise and shine. It is my year of celebration and not a year of mourning.

I am walking from connection to connection, from blessing to blessing, from protection to protection, from power to power, from victory to victory, in the Name of Jesus Christ.

Holy Spirit, all through this year, delight and lead all the affairs of my life, and that of my family, according to Your riches in glory.

In Jesus name.

Day 3: **Arise**

₁Arise, shine; for thy light is come, and the glory of the Lord is risen upon thee. – Isaiah 60:1

The first thing God wants us to do this year is to arise. Until we arise, we cannot shine.

To arise means to get up, stand up, jump up, leap up, spring up, and straighten up. We must get up from where we are now and begin to move towards where God wants us to be. This is the first instruction we must obey to shine this year.

To some of us, **ARISE** means to repent from a bad habit in our lives. To others, it means to let the past go, and to some, it means to get over your loss and move on.

WHAT DO YOU NEED TO ARISE FROM?

The first step to arising is to come to terms with yourself and ascertain where you are at the moment. The prodigal son came to his senses and then said, *I will arise* (Luke

15:17-18). That means he realized that something was wrong and that he needed to take practical steps to change his life.

Blind Bartimaeus arose and threw off his beggarly coat and ran to meet Jesus (Mark 10:49). For him that day, enough was enough. There was no going back to begging.

Sometimes we need to arise from our past before we can move on to our future. Sometimes we need to arise from our laziness. Sometimes we need to arise from wrong relationships and friendships, and sometimes it is low self-esteem that we must arise from.

But for us to shine, we must arise.

And there are times we do not know precisely where and what we must arise from. There are times we need the direction of the Holy Spirit to know exactly where we must arise from. That is why we need to come before God today and say, *"Lord, show me where I am now that I must arise from to shine this year, in Jesus name."*

PRAYERS/DECLARATIONS

Dear Heavenly Father, I thank You for Your plans for my life. You said that the thoughts You have for me are for peace, not of evil; of prosperity, not of poverty; to give me an expected end. May You be glorified forever and ever, in Jesus name.

I desire to arise and shine this year, Lord. I, therefore, pray, O Lord, show me where I am now that I must arise from. Show me relationships that I must quit. Show me sins I must confess and denounce. Show me habits I must break away from. Show me fences I must mend. Show me apologies I must make, and show me relationships I must heal by forgiveness, in Jesus name.

Today, Lord, I throw away the cloak of laziness. I surrender the coat of low self-esteem and self-pity. I give up the cover of excuses and fear. I put on the shield of faith and take on the mantle of purpose.

I speak to myself this day and declare: no more will I sit in darkness. I arise from now onwards and connect to

God's purpose for my life. I arise and connect to God's mercy and help. I arise and receive boldness to take every divine step ordained for my shining this year, in Jesus name.

May every spirit of slackness, negligence, and negative self-focus cease to exist in my life henceforth. May pride, arrogance, and self-dependence end in my life today. May all forms of evil thoughts, imaginations, and destructive strongholds wither from my spirit today.

I command my spirit to arise in wisdom, just as the prodigal son did, and go back to God's purpose for my life; I command my spirit to locate every step I must take to reconnect with God's destiny for me; I command my spirit to leave off every form of childishness, pettiness and focus on God's grand master plan for my life this year, in Jesus name.

O LORD, wherever and however I have forsaken my place of divine placement, I ask You for revelation and grace to retrace my steps this day. Show me any weakness in my life that is working with the devil to destroy my life, and help me by the Holy Spirit to surrender my weaknesses to You and receive Your strength to walk in victory over them this year, in Jesus' name.

It is written that while men slept, the enemy came and sowed tares (Matthew 13:25).

Heavenly Father, I pray this day that the Holy Spirit will wake me up from all forms of spiritual laziness and slumber. Whatever the enemy has planted in my life and family, in the past, as a result of my spiritual laziness and sleepiness, LORD, let them be uprooted and destroyed this day, in Jesus name.

Father Lord, open my eyes to see and understand what the enemy has broken in my life, career, family, and ministry; and help me in this season of waiting on You to demand Your total healing and restoration.

Anything that is making me powerless in the spiritual world, Lord Jesus Christ, take it out of my life today.

Every door I have opened out of ignorance, fear or doubt, that has enabled the devil to harass my life and family before now, I close them this day, in Jesus name.

From today, and all through this year, I declare that I have risen to shine, in Jesus name.

Day 4: **Shine**

"Arise, shine; For your light has come! And the glory of the Lord rises upon you." – Isaiah 60:1

The second thing, according to our anchor scripture, is to shine. But to shine, we need light. Without light, darkness will persist and even win.

Light in scripture symbolizes divine revelation, knowledge, direction, or discovery of what must be done.

If someone is sitting in darkness – a symbol of fear, failure, confusion, disgrace, poverty, wretchedness, persistent loss, persistent attacks, and so on. When the person decides to arise, the first thing he must do is to look for light or switch on the light. Without light, he will never know the way out of his darkness or dark spot.

Thankfully, God knew that this world would be covered with darkness – fear, failure, worry, confusion, attacks, and crimes – so He gave us light that will make us see ahead and protect ourselves. Today, God is reminding us of the importance of that light and telling us to go for it. That is the key to our shining amid the darkness.

WHAT DOES LIGHT MEANS TO YOU?

Light means *"understanding by revelation or insight what you need to do about a particular situation in your life or family that may have defied prayers, counseling, and every effort you have applied.* You cannot continue to do the same things you have done over the years and expect a different result. You need to change your approach this year. You need to change strategy. And to know what exactly needs to change, you need light.

Thankfully, the scripture says, *"For your light has come!"* This means that the Light you will need to walk out of your darkness is available. You will not need to travel or search too long for it. All you need is a genuine desire for light and asking God for it.

HOW DOES GOD GIVE US LIGHT?

First, we access divine light through the Word of God. The Bible says, ***"Your word is a lamp for my feet, a light on my path"*** (Psalm 119:105). From today, and all through this year, as you read the scriptures or meditate on the Word, or hear a teaching or preaching, desire and look for the light. In your spirit, it will drop, and you will know exactly what to do.

Some of the breakthroughs and successes I have experienced in life came through a revelation I saw through the Word. While on the Word, I could see in my spirit what I must do. After that, I got up and followed it up with action. Then I saw great results and miracles.

The light that comes through the Word shatters every form of darkness and opens tremendous doors.

Secondly, we access light through the Holy Spirit. For "...the Spirit searches all things, even the deep things of God. For who knows a person's thoughts except for their spirit within them? In the same way, no one knows the thoughts of God except the Spirit of God" (1 Corinthians 2:10-11)

The Holy Spirit is the custodian of God's mysteries; He is the revelator of secrets. You can trust Him to bring light into your darkness. He will show you precisely what needs to be done in any situation. He will instruct your heart either through a vision, dream, voice, inner witness, or whatever method that He deems fit. Let us ask Him for light this year.

PRAYERS/DECLARATIONS

Thank You, Lord, because I am confident that it is Your will for me to arise and shine this year. Thank You because my light has come, and Your glory has risen upon me.

I pray today, Lord, by the Holy Spirit, grant me access to Your light. As I read, study and listen to Your Word henceforth, show me things I need to do about my life and the issues confronting me.

This year, O Lord, instruct me and teach me in the way that I should go and guide me with Thine eye. I do not want to be like the horse or like the mule, which has no understanding, which must be harnessed with bit and bridle to stay on track.

Open my ears to hear; open my eyes to see, and open my heart to understand the path you have ordained for me this year, and what I must do to walk in the liberty I have through Jesus Christ, in Jesus name.

O Lord, I thank You because You have not allowed the battles that I faced all this while to swallow me. You have kept me from the attacks of the enemy. I am sure You are at work in my life to bring me complete recovery and victory all around.

If there be any instruction, direction, and guidance that I have ignored in the past, knowingly or unknowingly, which is now responsible for my being spoiled, plundered and trapped in holes; O LORD, please forgive me, and restore whatever the enemy has tampered in my life, family, and destiny, in Jesus name

Henceforth, LORD, I surrender to You completely. Guide me through thy Holy Spirit to remember everything You have said to me in the past that I need to obey. Teach me how to receive answers to all my prayers and have victory over the present circumstances confronting me, in Jesus name.

Satan, I reject your distractions from now onwards. I reject your lies and confusion in my mind. I bind you and command all your attacks and projections targeted at blinding me towards God's voice to me to be destroyed, in Jesus name.

Father, LORD, from today, inspire me with the right thoughts, ideas, and imaginations that will bring clarity to what You are leading me to do. Connect me with the right persons through which what you are telling me will be confirmed and ascertained, in Jesus name.

---

6. In the name of Jesus Christ, I decree today that the LORD orders my paths. I am walking in His direction for my life. I am taking back whatever has been stolen from me in the past.

By the Holy Spirit's revelation, I will know what I should do **(mention specific issues you need clarity on),** *and I receive grace to obey, in Jesus name.*

LORD, I pray, this year, even when I plan my ways in my heart, please direct my steps in Your will, and bring glory to Your Name through my life, for it is written that a man's heart may plan his way, but You LORD, directs his steps (Proverbs 16:9).

COMMIT YOUR PLANS TO THE LORD

Declare: *"God will show me profound mysteries beyond man's understanding because He knows all hidden things. He is light, and darkness does not stop Him. He will show me His secret and cause me to walk in His path because I fear him. And He will establish me in His Covenant, in Jesus name"*

Pray: *Heavenly Father, I thank You for the gift of the Holy Spirit who guides us into all truth, and bring to us all things You have said unto us. You are the One to whom no secret is hidden. I, therefore, ask You today to make known unto me the depths of this situation before me right now.....*(**mention specific things or areas you need His clarification and direction**) *in Jesus name*

O LORD, Remove from me any persistent buried grudges or half-acknowledged enmity against anyone, and every other thing that is blocking my spiritual vision.

Let every idol of personal opinions and conceptions present, consciously and unconsciously in my heart regarding this issue, be melted away by the fire of the Holy Spirit, in Jesus name.

O Lord, please give me the spirit of revelation and wisdom in the knowledge of you. Teach me what to do about this situation.

Yes, LORD, teach me the deep and secret things about this matter, in Jesus name.

Today LORD, I curse every spirit of spiritual blindness in my life. I curse the spirit of haste and impatience.

I decree and declare that I refuse to fall under the manipulation of spirits of confusion anymore.

I declare that I will no longer make foundational mistakes in my choices and decisions anymore, in the name of Jesus Christ.

O Lord, teach me to know that which is worth knowing.

To love that which is worth loving,

And to dislike whatsoever is not pleasing to Your eyes.

Make Your way plain before my face from now onwards and lead me in the path to take henceforth.

Lord, You are the One who reveals secret things. I now ask You to make known unto me Your choice for me in these issues before me. Through the Holy Spirit, Lord, open my eyes and help me to make the right decisions this year. Guide and direct me in knowing Your mind and thoughts,

In the name of Jesus Christ.

In the Almighty name of Jesus Christ, I bind the activities of ....

    i.   *Lust and ungodly infatuation*

    ii.   *Ungodly family pressure*

    iii.   *Demonic manipulation in dreams and visions.*

    iv.   *Negative soul ties and attachments to the wrong choice*

    v.   *Confusing revelations and dreams*

    vi.   *Ungodly and unprofitable suggestions*

    vii.   *Ungodly impatience.*

I decree that I will not miss the mark on these issues and in my life this year, in Jesus name.

Day 5: **You're Safe**

"For behold, the darkness shall cover the earth, and deep darkness the people; but the Lord will arise over you, and His glory will be seen upon you." – Isaiah 60:2

Darkness is a symbol of evil, fear, loss, death, terrorism, confusion, and pain. God is saying that even though darkness prevails in the world, He will be our light. The Psalmist confirms this in Psalm 91, where he says:

> ₅You shall not be afraid of the terror by night, nor of the arrow that flies by day, ₆Nor of the pestilence that walks in darkness, nor of the destruction that lays waste at noonday.

> ₇A thousand may fall at your side, and ten thousand at your right hand; but it shall not come near you.

> ₈ Only with your eyes shall you look, and see the reward of the wicked. ₉Because you have made the Lord, who is my refuge, even the Most High, your dwelling place. – Psalm 91:5-9

God is assuring you of His protection, preservation, and provision this year. Come boldly before Him today and declare His word of protection over your family, your loved ones and your life.

PRAYERS/DECLARATIONS

1. Psalm 91 (Prayerphrased)

₁*All through this year, I am dwelling in the secret place of the Almighty God. So I shall remain established under His shadow where no enemy can withstand His power.*

₂ *I will say of the Lord, He is my Refuge and my Fortress; my God, in Him I depend on, and in Him, I put my trust!*

₃*Every day in this year, God will deliver me from every trap of the enemy and from all deadly diseases that attack the world*

₄ He will shield me with His feathers, and under His arms shall I find refuge, for He is faithful always. He is my armor and my shield.

₅ Today, I declare that I shall not be afraid of the fears of the night, nor of the arrows and evil plots and slanders that happens during the day.

₆ I shall not fear the pestilence that threatens in darkness, nor of the destructions and sudden deaths that looms and lay waste at noonday.

₇ Even if a thousand falls at my side and ten thousand at my right hand, no evil shall come near me.

₈ I will only be a spectator over the attacks and punishments of the wicked.

₉ Today, I declare that the Lord is my refuge, and the Almighty God is my dwelling place... so ₁₀ there shall no evil befall me, nor any infection or calamity come near my dwelling.

11 For God's angels are under instruction to cover me, to escort and to defend and preserve me in all my ways. 12 They shall bear me up on their hands, and I will never dash my foot against a stone.

---

13 All through this year, if I encounter or step on lions and snakes, witches and wizards, or evil people, I will crush them under my foot because God is with me

14 He will deliver me continually from the intentions of the wicked; He will set me on high, because of His name; His mercy, love, and kindness will never forsake me, forever and ever.

---

15 This year, God will answer my prayers when I call on Him. He will be with at all times as He promised.

In troubles, He will be with me; He will deliver me and bring me to a place of honor, and 16 with long life will He satisfy me and show me His salvation, in Jesus name.

Amen.

---

2. Against the Powers Of Darkness

Heavenly Father,

I thank You for the victory that I have over the powers of satan through the death and resurrection of Jesus Christ.

Thank You for delivering us from the power of darkness, and translating us into the kingdom of Your dear Son, Jesus Christ, in whom we have redemption because of His sacrifice, resulting in the forgiveness of our sins and the cancellation of the penalty of our sins (Colossians 1:13-15).

O Lord, I pray this day, any man or woman who is posing as a friend in my life and family, but is secretly working for my downfall, Father expose their intentions and frustrate their activities this year, in Jesus name.

Father, give me the wisdom to recognize when I am walking towards the traps of men, and to be able to resist these traps.

May every agent of darkness assigned against my life this year become frustrated this day and bundled back into the abyss, in Jesus name.

―――――――――――――――――――――――――――――――

Blood of Jesus Christ, completely erase my name and my family from all forms of lineage curses and generational covenants.

I decree that by the Blood of Jesus Christ, myself, my family, my children, and my lineage, henceforth, belong to the covenant of salvation in Christ. We are no longer victims of evil blood covenants, in Jesus name.

―――――――――――――――――――――――――――――――

Father, in every area of my life, I claim the assistance, support, and help of Your angels assigned to protect and guide me this year. I release Your angels to go right now, and all through this year, and correct every negative information that the enemy has spread about me, in Jesus name.

Day 6: **A Positive Influence**

"Nations will come to your light, and kings to the brightness of your dawn." – Isaiah 60:3

Influence is the ability to make a strong impression in the perception of others around you, so much that they are forced to want to follow your path without your direct enticement. If someone influences someone else, they are changing the person in an indirect but significant way.

Recently, I began to talk about influence evangelism. That is, winning others to Christ without directly talking to them, but by influencing them with our results of faith and works, so much that they demand to serve our God.

Influence evangelism is, for me, the best way to win others to Christ.

Jesus talked about influence evangelism when He said, "Let your light so shine before men, that they may see your good works, and glorify your Father which is in heaven" (Matthew 5:16).

In today's verse, the Bible talks about nations and kings coming to the brightness of our dawn (or rising). Why would they do that?

1. Because we arose from where we were

2. Found God's light and are walking in it

3. So the darkness in the world didn't matter to us because as long as we are walking in the Light, we are covered by His glory.

Our influence, therefore, begins to speak so visibly that nations and kings take note and seek us out.

You cannot influence others to Christ if there is no difference between you and them. Neither will you attract them to seek God if your light is so dim that even you can barely see with it.

Today's prayer is a call for us to let our light shine this year in every aspect of our lives. In the office where we work, our light must shine; in the ministry, our light must shine; in our home, our light must shine; in our businesses, our light must shine.

PRAYERS/DECLARATIONS

Heavenly Father, make me a positive influence in my community this year. Wherever I go and whatever I do, Lord, empower me to strive for distinction.

I ask for the Spirit of excellence, competence, and effectiveness, Lord. Remind me always that You have called me to be the head and not the tail.

By the Holy Spirit, teach me how to be profitable in my career, business, family, and in my work for You.

May the spirits of laziness, procrastination, lack of commitment, worry, fear, and complaining, depart from my life this year, in Jesus name.

This year, O Lord, I decree that I will be committed to excellence. I will be productive and profitable in my commitments and my work. My labor will produce abundantly this year, in Jesus name.

O Lord, baptize me with grace and wisdom that will make me a positive influence in the lives of others this year. Use me to make life better for others in Jesus name.

I decree and declare that my light must shine this year. And through my light, others will also see light. Through my light, others will come to the saving grace of Jesus. Through my light, the works of darkness will be defeated in the lives of others, in the name of Jesus Christ.

This year, I must work the works of God in truth and in power. I will be an example of the abundant life and wisdom of God. I will distribute grace, wisdom, peace, and love to others in abundance this year.

I will be an instrument of encouragement to others this year. And as I sow encouragement to others, I will reap help, support, and encouragement also, in Jesus name

---

This year, O Lord, I come against the powers of depression, confusion of mind, fear, and doubt. I decree that the Lord is with me. He is my helper, my strength in weakness, and the lifter of my head. Therefore, I shall not fear the plans, threats, and intentions of mere mortals, in Jesus name.

This year, O LORD, help me to never dwell on my past failures, weaknesses, and mistakes. Help me to only focus on your love, wisdom, and the new things you are doing in my life and destiny, in Jesus name.

I speak to myself today and command myself to be confident in the LORD all through this year. I command myself to be bold and step out and walk in the purpose of God for my life, excelling in all areas of life, in Jesus name.

This year, O Lord, I decree that I am an overall victor. I reject all forms of victim/loser mentality. I decree that my victory in all aspects of life becomes real this year, in Jesus name.

Day 7: **Your Children & Your Home**

Lift up your eyes and see! For your sons and daughters are coming home to you from distant lands. – Isaiah 60:4

Originally, this scripture and its entire promises were made to the Israelites. It was a prophecy speaking about their restoration into the promised land. And Bible history shows that time, and again, it has happened exactly as God said.

But God's Word here also speaks to us as individuals. So while we note its significance to the nation of Israel, we must not fail to appreciate its implication to our personal lives as well.

LIFT YOUR EYES AND SEE

Every time God is planning something big, He needs our cooperation. He said to Abraham in Genesis 13:15, "I am giving all this land, as far as you can see..."

God is limited only to the depth and height of our sight. If we don't accept and see in advance what God is saying, we limit the manifestation of His blessings and promises in our lives.

Today, God is speaking about your home, about your family, and about your children. He says, "What do you see?"

God says that your children will come to you from afar. That is more like saying: they will be restored from prodigality. They will not be scattered. They will become the prayers you have prayed for them.

> **God says, "Begin to see your children in the light of my Word, not in the light of their present behaviors."**

They may not be acting right at the moment, but don't worry, your responsibility is to love, correct, and support. God is building them to Himself.

So today, our prayer focus is towards our families. We know that the devil's biggest attack area is the family system. But God has given us a Word that He is at work in our homes. There's no cause for alarm.

FOR MEDITATION

Psalm 128:3 - Your wife will be like a fruitful vine within your house; your children will be like olive shoots around your table.

1 Peter 4:8 - Above all, love each other deeply, because love covers over a multitude of sins.

Ecclesiastes 4:12 - "Though one may be overpowered, two can defend themselves. A cord of three strands is not quickly broken."

Ephesians 4:2-3 - "Be completely humble and gentle; Be patient, bearing with one another in love. Make every effort to keep the unity of the spirit through the bond of peace."

Psalm 34:3-9: Trust in the Lord and do good; dwell in the land and enjoy safe pasture.

4 Take delight in the Lord, and he will give you the desires of your heart.

5 Commit your way to the Lord;   trust in him, and he will do this:

₆ He will make your righteous reward shine like the dawn,   your vindication like the noonday sun.

₇ Be still before the Lord and wait patiently for him; do not fret when people succeed in their ways, when they carry out their wicked schemes.

₈ Refrain from anger and turn from wrath; do not fret—it leads only to evil.

₉ Those who are evil will be destroyed, but those who hope in the Lord will inherit the land.

PRAYERS AND DECLARATIONS

For Your Family

O Lord my Father, I thank You today for Your Word about my family and my children. Thank You that You are at work in my family and in the lives of my children.

Today, Lord, I begin to see my home in the light of Your Word and not in the light of anyone's behaviors. I see my spouse saved, humble and serving You. I see my children saved, blessed and serving you. I see my home, my family and every one of us reflecting Your glory forever and ever, in Jesus name.

Heavenly Father, You said it shall be unto me according to my faith. So I decree that my family is a center for peace, love, and excellence henceforth. I decree that the love of God oozes out of my home from this day forward, like never before. I decree that my family is a blessing to this generation, in Jesus name.

O Lord, make me Your ambassador in my home - always believing and trusting You, always setting an example of peace, love, and support for everyone, in Jesus name.

Father, may Your Spirit take charge of the lives of my family members (name them) henceforth. Turn our hearts to each other and to Your Love and grace.

Help each member of my family to be humble and gentle in our communications with each other; and to be patient, bearing with one another's mistakes in love – even when we're tired, frustrated, angry, or hurt.

Help us, Father, to make every effort to remain united in the Spirit in this home, in Jesus name.

O Lord Jesus Christ, I dedicate my family and home to You throughout this year. Rule and reign in our house. Be our Lord and Savior, in Jesus name.

For Your Marriage

Dear Heavenly Father, I come to YOU this day with all my heart. I recognize that You are the One who instituted marriage to further Your will here on earth. Thank You for my partner whom You have given to me.

Lord Jesus, I come to You today and completely surrender to You. I ask You to forgive me in every way I have tried to work out my relationship without You.

How often do I think that it is in my hand to make the best out of my partner. Lord, forgive my ignorance and negative thinking.

You said in 2 Chronicles 7:14 that if I humble myself and confess my faults, that You will forgive me and heal my land.

Lord, in this case, my land is my relationship. I confess my faults in thoughts, words, and actions in my relationship with my spouse and partner. Forgive me, cleanse me and let your mercy be made manifest in my marriage by the Blood of Jesus Christ.

Lord, I claim Your Forgiveness today. I claim Your grace and mercy to find help in my relationship, in Jesus name.

O Lord, I bring my partner before You today. I raise my relationship and marriage before Thee. O Lord, teach us to love You and to love and respect one another.

Help us to delight in You always. Help us to believe You at all times and trust Your work in our lives.

Draw us closer to You each day of our lives, Lord, both now and forever, in Jesus name.

Father, You said that as I delight myself in You, that You will give me the desires of my heart. That as I trust You, You will make my righteousness shine like the dawn.

Lord, I desire that You will prevail in my marriage and amplify Your love and understanding between me and my spouse, far more greater than it used to be.

Cause us to continue to find favor with each other continually. Take away strife between us and bind us once again in Your love, in Jesus name.

I speak right now to the spirits of anger, conflict, hate, alcohol, addiction, and indecency; I bind you demons and command you all to pack your belongings and leave my life and that of my partner right now.

I command all demons causing strife, anger, quarreling, misunderstanding, thoughts of indecency, addiction to negativity, and separation to go into the abyss and remain there bound forever and ever, in Jesus name.

I decree today that my partner and I are humble and serving the LORD. I decree that our hearts are arrested and bonded together in the spirit and in the physical.

This year, I decree that there is increased peace, love, romance, understanding, respect, and cooperation between my spouse and I, in Jesus name.

Day 8: **Prosperity From Above**

₅Your eyes will shine with joy, your hearts will thrill, for merchants from around the world will flow to you, bringing you the wealth of many lands.

₆Vast droves of camels will converge upon you, dromedaries from Midian and Sheba and Ephah too, bringing gold and incense to add to the praise of God.

₇The flocks of Kedar shall be given you, and the rams of Nabaioth for my altars, and I will glorify my glorious Temple in that day. – Isaiah 60: 5-7

God wants us to prosper financially. Our prosperity delights Him because it empowers us to do good works and share the love of Christ with the world.

According to God's word to us for the year, one of the areas we expect great supernatural intervention is in our finances. Today's verse gives us a picture of the abundance coming to our care after the order of God.

Close your eyes for a moment and imagine merchants (traders, businessmen and women) from around the world coming to you, bringing you the wealth of many lands. Imagine vast droves of camels converging upon you, dromedaries from Midian and Sheba, and Ephah too, bringing gold and incense to add to the praise of God in your life.

That's what you should expect – unusual wealth and accelerated financial breakthrough. So our focus in today's prayer is to declare God's power of wealth creation over our lives and to reject every plan of scarcity and invoke divine surplus.

DIVINE DIRECTION CREATES WEALTH

In Genesis chapter 26, there was a recession in the land. Isaac wanted to leave the country, but God appeared to him and told him to stay put and invest. He obeyed. The Bible then reports that "Isaac planted crops in that land and the same year reaped a hundredfold because the Lord blessed him. The man became rich, and his wealth continued to grow until he became very wealthy." (Genesis 26:12-13).

Divine direction is the most important key to wealth creation in the kingdom. This is the key lesson from Isaac's story of wealth in a time of recession.

To access the prosperity God has promised us this year, we must desire and pray for divine direction. There may be new ideas to explore, or some jobs to quit, or new businesses to start, or new areas and niches to venture into. We won't know until we are directed, and we won't be directed until we desire and seek for direction.

God's direction will unquestionably cause any land to be fruitful.

This is what we must pray for this year.

BE SPIRITUALLY ALERT

While praying for financial breakthrough, we must be spiritually alert because one way that God answers financial miracle breakthrough prayers is by dropping ideas or supernatural thoughts in our spirits. These may be new ideas on where to drop your CV, or persons to approach for business discussion, or outright new business ideas, or anything.

When these unplanned thoughts drop in your spirit, don't despise them. Recognize them and consider following their recommendations, for inside these divine thoughts are hidden our breakthroughs.

Remember Peter's experience in Luke 5. He had toiled all night without a single catch of fish. He and his colleagues were frustrated and confused and needed a breakthrough. Jesus came on board and after using his boat to preach, told him to cast his net again into the water.

At first, Peter tried to explain to Jesus that fishes don't show up when the water is hot and troubled. That it makes no sense trying to catch a fish during the day, from the same water where they couldn't find a single fish when the waters were quiet, and fishes were more ready to show up.

Nevertheless, he decided to prove to Christ that he (Peter) is right in his view by casting his net into the water. The bible says:

₆When they had done so, they caught such a large number of fish that their nets began to break. ₇So they signaled their partners in the other boat to come and help them, and they came and filled both boats so full that they began to sink.

That's more like saying, "Peter, I know you've failed in this business. But go ahead and try again."

One thing about divine instructions or the ideas that God puts in our hearts through our prayers and fasting is that they contain the answers we seek. That is why it is highly encouraged that you recognize these divine thoughts, write them down, and follow them.

FOR MEDITATION AND CONFESSION

Psalm 35:27 - *Let them shout for joy, and be glad, that favor my righteous cause: yea, let them say continually, Let the LORD be magnified, which hath pleasure in the prosperity   of   his   servant.*

Deuteronomy 8:18 - *But thou shalt remember the LORD thy God: for it is he that giveth thee power to get wealth, that he may establish his covenant which he* *sware unto thy fathers, as [it is] this day.*

Philippians 4:19 - But my God shall supply all your need according to his riches in glory by Christ Jesus.

---

3 John 1:2 - Beloved, I wish above all things that thou mayest prosper and be in health, even as thy soul prospereth.

---

2 Corinthians 9:8 - And God is able to make all grace abound toward you; that ye, always having all sufficiency in all things, may abound to every good work:

Psalms 1:3 - And he shall be like a tree planted by the rivers of water, that bringeth forth his fruit in his season; his leaf also shall not wither, and whatsoever he doeth shall   prosper.

PRAYERS AND DECLARATIONS

Heavenly Father, thank You for it is Your will that I prosper and be in good health.

Thank You because I am certain that this year is a year of abundance of wealth for me and my household.

I give You praise because You delight in the prosperity of Your people.

I give You praise because all through this year, You will supply our needs according to Your riches in Christ Jesus.

Receive my praise today in Jesus name.

O Lord, how often do I think that prosperity, money, and success is by my efforts and decisiosn alone.

Lord, I come to You this day and confess my ignorance and pride. Forgive me for not giving You the ultimate place in my finances in the past. Forgive me, Lord. Let Your mercy prevail over me this day, in Jesus name.

O Lord, by the Blood of Jesus Christ, I receive forgiveness from any form of greed and financial impropriety in the past.

Lord Jesus, throughout this year and beyond, let Your Blood speak for me financially from this moment, in Jesus name.

It is written in Job 36:11, that if I obey and serve God, that I will spend my days in prosperity and my years in plenty.

Lord, I desire to serve and obey you from this day forward. I come to You right now and ask for the grace to be a doer of the Word on finances and in every aspect of life, in Jesus name.

Dear Holy Spirit, I come to You and ask that You make me willing and obedient to the WORD of God henceforth, according to Isaiah 1:19, so that I may eat the good things of the land.

Holy Spirit, uproot every seed of greed and disobedience from me this day, in Jesus name.

Father, from this year on, make me a blessing in my community. Make me a light that supports those who are in need, for it is written that when I give, You will command men to give back to me.

Inspire me to give and to give joyfully without regrets all the days of my life, in Jesus name.

This year Holy Spirit, motivate me and help me to honor the Lord with my resources and finances so that my barns will be full and overflowing with harvest... as it is written in Proverbs 3:9-10: ***"Honor the Lord from your wealth and from the first of all your produce; so your barns will be filled with plenty and your vats will overflow with new wine.***

O Lord, I desire to obey this Word. So give me the enablement and direction to obey at all times, in Jesus name.

Today, I stand in authority in the name of Jesus Christ right now.

I command every demon working against my business, my career, and my finances to collapse, be bound and cast into the abyss, in Jesus name.

It is written in Matthew 16:19 that whatsoever I bind here on earth is bound in heaven, and whatsoever I loose here on earth is loosed in heaven.

I, therefore, bind every spirit of poverty, lack, frustration, and loss. I cast them into the abyss from today, in Jesus name.

O Lord, based on Your Word, we have authority here on earth, and according to Mark 11:23, we can speak to the mountain, and it will have to obey us.

So, devil, I speak to you in the name of Jesus Christ, I command you to take your hands off my finances right now in the Name of Jesus.

I speak to the mountain of Lack and Want. I command you to be removed and cast into the sea from this day, in the name of Jesus Christ.

Today and all the days of this year, I command the abundance of God, and all that rightfully belongs to me now to locate me in Jesus name.

I declare today that I cast all my cares and money worries over on You Lord. I will not worry anymore, neither will I fret.

I have peace, and I'm enjoying God's supplies every day of my life, in Jesus name.

It is written that angels are ministering spirits sent to minister unto the heirs of salvation.

Therefore, Lord, I ask that Your angels of goodness, love and success minister to all my needs this year, in the name of Jesus Christ.

Wherever my finances are, whoever is connected to my financial breakthroughs, O Lord, let your angels reconnect them to me this day, and this year.

As I step out to work on my business or career, Lord Jesus, men, and women will bring me favor, in Jesus name.

Father, give me the power to create wealth this year. As it is written that You give us power to create wealth.

I ask for the power, wisdom, and guidance to create wealth in my life. In Jesus name.

Lord, I ask You today for ideas, I ask You for inspiration and divine strategies to turn my career around and grow my pursuit into a global brand.

Show me secrets hidden from men and help me to unleash Your full potential in what I am doing at the moment, in Jesus name.

O Lord, make me an employer of labor so that I will be a blessing to others and fulfill the covenant of Abraham which I inherit in Christ Jesus. Direct me to men and materials that You assigned to bring me into my place of financial and business dominion before the world began, in Jesus name.

Holy Spirit, You are my teacher. I ask You to teach me how to be profitable in business and career this year. Teach me to become a shining light in my pursuits. Open my eyes to the right job opportunities and profitable business ventures, in Jesus name.

Thank You, Father, for Your Word in Psalm 1:3, which says that I am like a tree planted by the riverside. Whatever I do, prospers.

May prosperity and wealth fill my dwelling place this year, in Jesus name.

This year, merchants from around the world are coming to me, bringing me the wealth of many lands. Vast droves of camels are converging upon me, dromedaries from the four corners of the earth are bringing gold and incense to add to the praise of God in my life.

It is written in 1 Corinthians 9: 8 that God is able to make all grace abound toward me; that I, always having all sufficiency in all things, may abound to every good work.

Therefore, Lord, I decree that this year, I have all sufficiency in all things, and I lack nothing. I decree that the grace of God is causing me to abound in every good work, in Jesus name.

It is written in Psalm 112:3 that wealth and riches will be in my house, and his righteousness endures forever.

So I decree that my house shall be filled with wealth and riches this year, in Jesus name

God has given me the power to get wealth. I'm blessed in the field. I am blessed going in and going out. I have the favor of God.

Favor, breakthrough, success, money and every good thing comes to me from this day, in Jesus name.

Day 9: **Uncommon Favor**

₁₀"The sons of foreigners shall build up your walls, and their kings shall minister to you; for in My wrath I struck you, but in My favor I have had mercy on you.

₁₁Therefore your gates shall be open continually; they shall not be shut day or night, that men may bring to you the wealth of the Gentiles, and their kings in procession.

₁₂For the nation and kingdom which will not serve you shall perish, and those nations shall be utterly ruined. - Isaiah 60:10-12

In today's reading, God shows us a picture of uncommon favor – a favor that causes the sons of foreigners to build up our walls, and their kings minister to us. The favor that causes our gates to be open continually and never shut so that even unbelievers will bring wealth to us.

The favor that punishes groups or individuals that refuse to acknowledge God's hand in our lives, and serve us.

That's an uncommon favor. And it is part of God's package for us this year.

THE REALITY OF FAVOR

Yes, God loves us all and does not show favoritism. He welcomes us all equally and gifts us from His depth of love. But there is still something called favor. His favor is not partiality or bias. It is simply his approval and support and unquestionable preference based absolutely on His eternal purpose.

For instance, when the angel appeared to Mary, he said to her, *"...Hail, thou that art highly favored, the Lord is with thee: blessed art thou among women"* (Luke 1:28). She was not the only virgin in Israel. But God's favor found her, and today, the rest is history.

Divine favor can catapult a man from obscurity to limelight in just a few hours. Favor can open strange doors and cause you to be preferred above all others. It can cause unusual recommendation and upliftment that wows many and angers a lot of others.

Please understand this: Favor is real. You may not like the subject, but it is what it is. You can't do anything about it. In life, it will continue to separate people.

Today, God recommends Israel to the world. Hate or like them; it doesn't make any difference. They are God's preferred nation where His very presence and throne is established. If you fight them, you are fighting God Himself.

God's favor turns a little one into a mighty nation. His favor makes a shepherd boy with no qualification to become the greatest king of a nation. His favor picks a street hustler and turns him into a mighty judge and leader. His favor makes a hopeless prostitute become a great grandmother of the Messiah.

There were many inmates in that cell, but Joseph found favor in the sight of the prison warden because God's favor was with him. What made Esther the preferred over the other beauty contestants was God's favor at work in her life, not really because she was more qualified or more trained or more beautiful than the other girls.

Please don't question the reality of favor, and don't fight yourself over it. Instead, desire and pray for it. And when you spot it in someone's life, celebrate it. That's how to key into it.

HOW TO PROVOKE DIVINE FAVOR

The scripture gives us hints on how we can attract divine favor in our lives. Let's see some of these virtues:

1. Believe in favor: You cannot attract what you fight and repel in your mind. Yes, you may not understand the dynamics of divine favor, but don't fight it. God's favor is real.

2. Love God: Love God with all your heart, soul, and body. You cannot attract divine favor if you despise God. Pray today for a baptism of the Spirit of Love for God and the kingdom.

3. Love People and Be Faithful: Proverbs Chapter 3:1-4 says, "My son, do not forget my teaching, but keep my commands in your heart, for they will prolong your life many years and bring you peace and prosperity. *Let love and faithfulness never leave you; bind them around your neck, write them on the tablet of your heart*. ₄ Then you will win favor and a good name in the sight of God and man.

Pour out your life towards empowering others. God's favors flow back to anyone who cares for others. Ruth found favor with Boaz because of her works. She received more than she asked for, exceptional treatment, security, more than enough.

4. Hate what God hates: The Ephesian church had one thing for which God counted in their favor: they hated what God hates (Rev. 2:6 NIV). When you hate what God hates, you'll have favor roundabout.

> 16 These six things the Lord hates, yes, seven are an abomination to Him: 17 A proud look, a lying tongue, hands that shed innocent blood, 18 a heart that devises wicked plans, feet that are swift in running to evil, 19 a false witness who speaks lies, and one who sows discord among brethren. - Proverbs 6:16-19

This list is not an attempt to name what God hates but a statement to confirm that God does hate some things. I believe that the thing that God hates the most, which is capable of stopping His favor in our lives, is disobedience. That is why we must prayerfully repent of every form of disobedience and ask God for a new baptism of the Spirit that strives to obey Him at all times.

5. Be a Cheerful Giver: The popular saying that givers never lack is true. The Bible says, *"Give, and it will be given to you: good measure, pressed down, shaken together, and running over will be put into your bosom. For with the same measure that you use, it will be measured back to you"* (Luke 6:38).

This is one powerful law of life that always works for or against us: We reap what we sow – good or bad.

If you desire mercy, sow mercy and keep sowing; you will eventually start reaping mercy.

If you desire help, start helping others and never stop doing that. With time, you will begin to receive help even when you didn't ask.

If you need favor, start sowing **favor seeds** in the lives of others. With time, favor will find its way back to you.

Sow prayer seeds in the lives of others. That is, pray for the needs of others. With time, the prayers you make for them, you will also start seeing the answers in your own life.

The law of giving works because it is founded on God's universal principle of living.

6. Desire to Live a Righteous Life: It is true that we cannot attain righteousness through our efforts. Our righteousness is of God through Christ Jesus. However, we cannot live carelessly without consequences. We must trust God's grace every day to empower us to walk in righteousness and holiness.

God defends the righteous and surrounds him with favor. The Bible says, *11 But let all those rejoice who put their trust in You; Let them ever shout for joy, because You defend them; Let those also who love Your name be joyful in You. 12 For You, O Lord will bless the righteous; with favor You will surround him as with a shield* (Psalm 5:11-12).

7. Be Humble; Detest Pride: 5 Likewise you younger people, submit yourselves to your elders. Yes, all of you be submissive to one another, and be clothed with humility, for "God resists the proud, but gives grace to the humble." 6 Therefore humble yourselves under the mighty hand of God, that He may exalt you in due time (1 Peter 5:5-6)

8. Love Honesty; Detest Deception: Joseph found favor with Potiphar because he could be trusted.

> Joseph found favor in his eyes and became his attendant. Potiphar put him in charge of his household, and he entrusted to his care everything he owned - Genesis 39:4.

Even though we live in a world of fast everything, integrity still pays. God honors reliability and faithfulness with favor. *"The Lord detests dishonest scales, but accurate weights find favor with Him"* (Proverbs 11:1).

9. Live a Joyful & Grateful Life: A grateful heart is a fruitful life. Never let anything tamper with your joy and thankfulness. The Bible says,

> ₃ Therefore with joy, you will draw water from the wells of salvation. ₄And in that day you will say:

> "Praise the Lord, call upon His name; declare His deeds among the peoples, make mention that His name is exalted.

> ₅ Sing to the Lord, for He has done excellent things; this is known in all the earth. - Isaiah 12:3-5

Gratitude and joy are twins and they work hand in hand. If you are grateful, you will be joyful. And if you are joyful, you will be grateful.

Always challenge yourself to be in joy, no matter the problems you're going through. With joy and a grateful heart, you will draw favor from the wells of salvation.

10. Prayer: Prayer is another powerful key that can unlock divine favor. Jabez' life was full of ill luck, failure, and confusion. One day he arose and told himself, *enough is enough.* Then he prayed and asked God to change his story and enlarge His coast. And God answered his prayers. He became more honorable than his brethren.

You can genuinely ask God to release favor in your life. You can ask Him to stop the works of disfavor in your life and make you a child that favor speaks for. And He will answer your prayers.

PRAYERS AND DECLARATIONS

Read These Promises

Psalms 5:12 - For thou, LORD, wilt bless the righteous; with favor wilt thou compass him as with a shield.

Psalms 102:13 - Thou shalt arise, and have mercy upon Zion: for the time to favor her, yea, the set time, is come.

Psalm 23:5-6 – 5 You prepare a table before me in the presence of my enemies; You anoint my head with oil; my cup runs over. 6 Surely goodness and mercy shall follow me all the days of my life, and I will dwell in the house of the Lord forever.

Psalm 30:5 - For His anger is but for a moment, His favor is for life; weeping may endure for a night, but joy comes in the morning.

Numbers 6:25-26 (TLB) - May the Lord bless and protect you; may the Lord's face radiate with joy because of you; may he be gracious to you, show you his favor, and give you his peace.

Pray

Heavenly Father, I thank You because this year, I shall walk in divine favor in every aspect of my life in Jesus name.

Thank You because Your plan for us this year encompasses favor roundabout. Be glorified because Your Word is yea and amen.

Lord, *I agree with Thy Word that the sons of foreigners shall build up my walls this year, and their kings shall minister to me.*

I agree with You O Lord that my days of been stuck and struck are over. From this day on, I will walk continually in Your favor because Your mercy is abundant towards me.

My gates shall be open continually; they shall not be shut day or night, that men may bring to me the wealth of the Gentiles, and their kings in procession, in Jesus name.

This year, nations and kingdoms will serve me. Anyone ordained to support and help me in any way will be supernaturally connected to me this year, in the name of Jesus Christ.

From today onwards, I declare that I receive uncommon and unlimited favor and breakthrough, in every aspect of my life.

This year, my joy shall multiply every day. Nothing shall be impossible for me because I am in Christ, and through him, I can do all things.

O Lord, throughout this year, stir my spirit to walk in Your love and to show genuine concern and kindness to others. Move me every day to hate what You hate and to be a cheerful giver, always sharing from Your abundance without grudges or fears, in Jesus name.

Lord, help me to pursue after righteousness and holiness; help me to walk before You this year in humility; uproot pride and arrogance from me; and baptize me with the Spirit of gratitude and joy, all the days of my life, in Jesus name.

This year, favor will reign in my life. By the Holy Spirit, I shall always be at the right place and at the right time.

I will no longer miss opportunities for promotion and lifting, in the name of Jesus Christ.

I hereby dismantle every spiritual opposition, curse, covenant, and incantation speaking disfavor, delay, and disgrace, in my life and family.

I put an end to all attacks creating near success syndrome, opposition at the edge of a breakthrough, and unnecessary hatred for me, in Jesus name.

I command all my past rejections to turn into open doors for me this year. Wherever I go, may God's favor speak on my behalf, in Jesus name.

O Lord, bless the works of my hands this year and be glorified through my prosperity. Make me a profitable Christian whose testimonies bring others to the saving grace of Jesus Christ, in Jesus name.

Father, open my eyes to recognize all of the untapped potentials you've blessed me with and help me not to take the blessings and favor you'll bless me with for granted in the name of Jesus Christ.

Precious Holy Spirit, stir my heart to draw close to You this year through daily meditation of Your Word. Give me clarity on the excellent opportunities at my disposal, in the name of Jesus.

Today, I speak to my mind to focus.

I speak to my mind to reject worry and self-pity.

I speak to my mind to reject every form of procrastination and laziness.

I welcome every labor designed to provoke the supernatural release of abundance into my life and family this year, in Jesus name.

I am clothed with the garment of favor this year. I am finding favor before God and before men every day. I am excelling in the plans and purposes of God for my life continually, in Jesus name

---

Today, I speak to all forms of fear and doubt in my life. I command them to end this moment.

I reject every attitude of timidity and claim a mind of boldness.

I banish anxiety and stress in my life throughout this year, in the name of Jesus Christ.

O Lord, open my eyes to recognize every relationship that is projected from the pit of hell to sabotage Your plans for my life and keep me in the pit of confusion and sorrow. Help me, Lord, to break free from those relationships, in Jesus name.

Lord, let your peace that surpasses all understanding saturate my mind, body, and soul this year, in Jesus name

---

Lord, I thank You because You are causing everyone and everything to work for my good. I thank You for causing me to be at the right place at the right time this year.

I thank You, Lord, for causing people to want to help me this year.

Thank You for blessing me with creativity; thank You for causing me to make good decisions with a clear mind, in Jesus name.

Today, I claim Psalm 84:11, that God is blessing me with favor and honor, and no good thing will He withhold from me.

Thank You, Lord, for Your favor today and every day, not because of who I am but because of who You are and whose child I am.

In Jesus name I pray.

Day 10: **Pray For Others**

Every believer is a partner with God in the business of saving others. We're saved to save others. The ministry of reconciliation is for us all, not for pastors, prophets, and evangelists.

> 17 Therefore, if anyone is in Christ, he is a new creation; old things have passed away; behold, all things have become new.

> 18 Now all things are of God, who has reconciled us to Himself through Jesus Christ and has given us the ministry of reconciliation. -2 Corinthians 5:17-18

If you're confused about what God is calling you to do, start by accepting that you have received a ministry of reconciliation from Him. Then begin to look for avenues to share the love of Christ with your community of influence. As you stay faithful with what is already revealed, what is not revealed will become revealed.

There is always something we can all do in our capacities to urge others to accept the salvation of the Lord Jesus Christ. Heartfelt prayer is one of those things.

So today's prayer will be focused on praying for the salvation of others. Come to God in humility and sincerely pray for persons in your family, neighborhood, or community that needs Jesus.

We're not going to pray some general prayers of, "Lord, save these people in this community." No. We're going to list names of few persons on paper and pray for their genuine salvation.

Jesus said:

> I tell you that in the same way, there will be more rejoicing in heaven over one sinner who repents than over ninety-nine righteous persons who do not need to repent - Luke 15:7.

Let us join in creating joy in heaven by genuinely praying for the salvation and healing of others.

WHAT TO DO

Write out names of people you'll be praying for their salvation today, and fill the blank spaces in the prayers below with these names.

FOR MEDITATION

Matthew 18:14- *"Even so it is not the will of your Father who is in heaven that one of these little ones should perish."*

2 Peter 3:9 - "The Lord is not slack concerning His promise, as some count slackness, but is longsuffering toward us, not willing that any should perish but that all should come to repentance."

1 Timothy 2:3-4 - "This is good, and pleases God our Savior, who wants all people to be saved and to come to a knowledge of the truth."

Acts 16:31 - "Believe in the Lord Jesus, and you will be saved, along with everyone in your household."

Luke 11:5-10 - Then Jesus said to them, *"Suppose you have a friend, and you go to him at midnight and say, 'Friend, lend me three loaves of bread; a friend of mine on a journey has come to me, and I have no food to offer him.'*

And suppose the one inside answers, 'Don't bother me. The door is already locked, and my children and I are in bed. I can't get up and give you anything.'

I tell you, even though he will not get up and give you the bread because of friendship, yet because of your shameless audacity[a] he will surely get up and give you as much as you need.

"So I say to you: Ask, and it will be given to you; seek, and you will find; knock, and the door will be opened to you.

For everyone who asks receives; the one who seeks finds; and to the one who knocks, the door will be opened.

PRAYER FOR SALVATION

O LORD, I Thank You because You do not want me, my family, my children, and these people I have here on my list to perish. Thank You, Lord, because You want us all to be saved.

This is the assurance I have in YOU that as I pray, I receive answers. In Jesus name.

Today O Lord, I declare that these shall be saved and come to the knowledge of the truth in Christ Jesus.

Let Your power of salvation visit the following people, Lord. Visit --------------------wherever they are right now. Visit them in the name of Jesus Christ.

Father Lord, I ask that out of Your unlimited resources You will empower -------------------- with the inner strength to accept Jesus as their Lord and Savior, in Jesus name.

Cause .... to be planted deep in the Love of Christ. Let them be rooted deep in Your love and comprehend with all of God's people the extravagant dimensions of Your love, in Jesus name.

Today, O Lord, I come against the spirit of rebellion in the lives of ----------------in Jesus name. I cast out every spirit of stubbornness and resistance; I command these anti-salvation spirits to be drowned in the abyss in the Mighty name of Jesus Christ.

Satan, I speak to you as one with authority from God to stop your works here on earth. I command you to lose your grips on the lives of ------------------------ right now, in Jesus name.

Wherever you are........................., I decree today that Jesus sets free, you are therefore free indeed. You are no longer under the influence of Satan and sin, in Jesus name.

I command .... to receive an encounter with Jesus Christ today. Receive a supernatural revelation of the person of Christ and be rooted in His Love henceforth, in the name of Jesus Christ.

I decree today that because .... are connected to me, and I believe in Jesus Christ and His Love, you are saved from sin to serve the living God through Christ Jesus, in Jesus name.

O Lord, my Father, I confess with Your Word that............. are saved and serving You, in Jesus name.

PRAYER FOR THE SICK

There are many sick people around you and in the hospitals. You may know some by name. Today, come before God and present them in prayers. Pray for God's healing power to be released into their lives.

> How God anointed Jesus of Nazareth with the Holy Ghost and with power: who went about doing good and healing all that were oppressed of the devil; for God was with him. - Acts 10:38

In the blank spaces, fill in the names of the persons you are praying for.

Dear heavenly Father, it is Your will to heal us and to walk in divine health. The price for our healing has been paid on the cross by Your Son, Jesus Christ.

So Father, as I pray for.................................this day, I am confident that Your healing power will be made manifest for their healing and deliverance from the sickness and pain tormenting them, in Jesus name.

O Lord, I stand in the gap now and ask for forgiveness for .... By the Blood of Jesus, I claim forgiveness from any sin and disobedience that has brought or empowered sickness to operate in the lives of........................in Jesus name.

Lord, according to Your Word, You forgive our sins and heal our diseases (Psalm 103:3). Therefore, I ask for forgiveness and total healing for .... in Jesus name.

I speak to the demons perpetrating illness in the lives of .... I command you demons to get out of their bodies this moment and be drowned in the abyss, in Jesus name.

As it is written, our bodies are the temple of the Holy Spirit. The bodies of .... are the temple of the Holy Spirit.

Therefore, you demons of affliction, pain, and defilement, pack your loads, and leave now. I cast you all into the bottomless pit, in Jesus name.

I hereby declare the bodies of .... as the temples of the Holy Spirit. I anoint them with oil now and decree complete healing and restoration of health, in the name of Jesus Christ.

O Lord, I ask that angels will carry out a spiritual surgery on .... today and bring them total healing, in Jesus name

---

I decree that ....will prosper and be in good health, even as their soul prospers in the Lord, in Jesus name.

Thank You, Jesus, for healing ....and causing them to walk in divine health. Your work is permanent. Everything you do is perfect.

Thank You Jesus.

Day 11: **No More Witchcraft**

Culled from the book, <u>Prayers to Destroy Witchcraft</u>

"And he made his children pass through the fire in the valley of the son of Hinnom: also he observed times, and used enchantments, and used witchcraft, and dealt with a familiar spirit, and with wizards: he wrought much evil in the sight of the LORD, to provoke him to anger." - **2 Chron 33:6**

Today, let us take authority against all practices and works of witchcraft against our lives and families or witchcraft activities projected against the year.

Witchcraft is the use of power gained from evil spirits or demons to inflict harm, foretell events, control people or things, deceive, or conjure something. It can also include the ability to control the powers of nature or someone else.

There's no difference between witchcraft, sorcery, divination, and magic. They all involve communicating with evil spirits and using their guidance to create good or bad situations, negative or positive experiences.

The following words and their practices mean the same thing as witchcraft: magic (black magic, white magic), sorcery, divination, black arts, occultism, wizardry, witchery, witching, necromancy (communicating with the dead), voodooism, voodoo, hoodoo, palm reading, Wicca, natural magic, makutu; rarethaumaturgy, theurgy, the old religion, demonry, diablerie, sortilege, medium, astrology, new ageism, etc.

All of these and their accomplishments are witchcraft and attract the same divine judgment and consequences. They are not just some form of old religion or nature worship. The Bible forbids them and declares them as taboos.

> 9 "When you come into the land which the Lord your God is giving you, you shall not learn to follow the abominations of those nations. 10 There shall not be found among you anyone who makes his son or his daughter pass through the fire, or one who practices witchcraft, or a soothsayer, or one who interprets omens, or a sorcerer, 11 or one who conjures spells, or a medium, or a spiritist, or one who calls up the dead.

12 For all who do these things are an abomination to the Lord, and because of these abominations the Lord your God drives them out from before you. 13 You shall be blameless before the Lord your God. 14 For these nations which you will dispossess listened to soothsayers and diviners; but as for you, the Lord your God has not appointed such for you. – (Deut.18:9-14)

Wikipedia, dictionaries, and witches may argue with you that witchcraft means something else. But God says that all forms of witchcraft are evil. I would rather listen to God than the world.

TYPES OF WITCHCRAFT

1. Ignorant (Blind) Witchcraft

Ignorant or blind witchcraft involves the practice of witchcraft without knowing what one is doing. Those who practice modern-day magic, and use it as fun, are practicing witchcraft unknowingly. Those who are buying books, courses, and tutorials, learning and trying different witchcraft essentials, like invocations, casting spells, magic,   air dance, fire dance, disappearing, conjuring things, etc. are involving themselves in witchcraft unknowingly.

Those who are joining secret societies, Eastern Star, Freemasons, Lodge, and so on, are also involving in witchcraft. Yes, one may see these organizations as just a group for socialization, learning, and personal improvement. However, their basic tenets of faith deny the deity of Jesus Christ and the Trinity. So whatever they are doing as benefits are just a cover-up for what they are in reality. Membership in them is, before God, a form of witchcraft.

Consulting fortune-tellers, sorcerers, necromancers, spiritists, palm readers, and magicians for some solution to life problems is also another way to involve in witchcraft unknowingly. Note that just because you have a problem and needed help, and so consults these mediums does not exonerate you from witchcraft. The Bible warns us against seeking means other than God through Jesus Christ for spiritual guidance and solution.

Whether one knows it or not while practicing witchcraft, the Bible clearly warns against witchcraft, in fact, often pronouncing harsh judgments for those who practice it.

2. Intentional Witchcraft

These are hardcore witches who use the practice of witchcraft to hurt others. They were either initiated into witchcraft by their earlier generations or through some contact with other witches. Either way, they are carrying out their acts intentionally. Their goal is to steal, kill and destroy. They may have been promised considerable rewards in their witchcraft covens and worship centers if they do more harm to their family members and to others.

These types of witches act upon the instruction and lies of the devil to perpetrate a lot of wickedness in the society, albeit secretly. We can destroy the limitations raised against us by this kind of witchcraft only with serious warfare prayers.

3. People Possessed With the Spirit of Witchcraft

The Bible references this class of witchcraft under the works of the flesh in Galatians 5: 19 -20:

*₁₉Now the actions of the flesh are manifest, which are these: Adultery, fornication, uncleanness, lasciviousness, ₂₀Idolatry, **witchcraft**, hatred, variance, emulations, wrath, strife, seditions, heresies.*

People whose attitudes hurt others practice this type of witchcraft. They are shown in the following ways:

- Bullying others

- Gossip

- Talking down on others

- Murder

- Intimidation

- Lack of empathy

- Narcissism

People who display these tendencies are unknowingly exhibiting witchcraft. The spirit of witchcraft is using them because witchcraft is about suppression, wickedness, and intimidation.

If you're in a relationship or working with someone who treats you like you're nobody, suppresses your views and demands your worship (directly or indirectly) as a way to get along, then this person is under the influence of witchcraft spirit. He or she may not be the real problem. You have to take authority against the spirit of witchcraft and break the control.

4. Charismatic Witchcraft

Charismatic witchcraft is exercising control over other Christians by leaders or anyone within the church, using personal prophecy or visions or other methods. Its intent revolves around domination, intimidation, manipulation, monetary profit, and emotional blackmail.

Many innocent Christians are suffering from one kind of affliction or the other because they submitted themselves to spiritual wolves in one way or the other. Not until recently when the LORD began to open my eyes did I start learning the danger posed by these lazy, pretentious, demonic men, who often pose as men and women of God. Beyond the risk of leading people away from the LORD, these wolves can also be a gateway for the imposition of spiritual obstacles against God's people.

These men and women come with enticing words, visions, and prophecies, and it's mostly difficult to decipher their real intent on a first look. They give visions and prophecies and lure ignorant Christians to their bidding. That is why we are warned not be carried away by prophecies and visions, especially prophecies and visions that don't have any Biblical basis.

No doubt, we are in a prophetic age. This is the age of the spirit of visions and prophecy. But we have to observe it because Satan too has trickily gotten involved.

Most times, the ultimate goal of these demonic men is their belly - to make a profit. So even in the visions and prophecies they give, there are no real solutions in them, but just monetization opportunities.

Am I against spiritual gifts, visions, prophecies, and seeing in the spirit?

Absolutely no.

But we have to discern all spirits as the Bible says. Not just because of the dangers so visible as I've shared, but because these prophecies and visions and what follows them have the potential of eventually becoming a source of satanic oppressions against a person.

5. Self-Witchcraft

Rebellion is willful disobedience to God's revealed voice, instruction, leading, and direction for one's life. The Bible considers this as equivalent to witchcraft. That's because the person tries to witchcraft (control) God to work in some way different from how God is leading. This was the primary reason for Saul's rejection as the king of Israel. 1 Samuel 15:23 says:

"For rebellion is as the sin of witchcraft, and stubbornness is as iniquity and idolatry. Because thou hast rejected the word of the LORD, he hath also rejected thee from being king."

Rebellion was also what led to Jonah being swallowed by a fish. He would have been destroyed if not that he repented in the fish's belly.

One thing about the sin of willfully disobeying God's revealed voice to you is that no one will have the solution to your problem or situation. You'll pray and pray, make confessions, sow seeds, but will not get help and answers because you are trying to get God to move in other ways different from His direction, which has been revealed to you, and which you know. It's only in repentance and humble submission that you'll get help and answers.

PRAYERS

Against Witchcraft

Heavenly Father, You have decreed that whatever I bind on earth will be bound in heaven, and whatever I loose on the earth will be loosed in heaven, and that if two of us on the earth agree about anything we ask for, it will be done for us exactly as we agreed (Matthew 18:18-19).

Today, Heavenly Father, I agree with Jesus. I agree with the Holy Spirit. And I agree with Your WORD.

I have authority and power over the spirits of witchcraft, Jezebel, wickedness, and disfavor. I have dominion over the decisions and activities of the forces of darkness at all levels

As I stand in this perfect agreement and pray and confess this day, I accept my victory over witchcraft and their works in my life and family this year, in Jesus name.

O Lord, there can be no two kings over my life and family. There can be no two masters and influencers over my destiny and my family.

Jesus Christ is the only Lord of my life, my destiny, and my family. He is the only One with the right to access and direct my thoughts, my family, and my destiny.

So I reject every form of authority of the devil and the witchcraft world over my life and family this year and forever, in Jesus name.

I plead the Blood of Jesus Christ right now over my spirit, soul, and body.

I plead the Blood of Jesus Christ over my home, my family, and my neighborhood.

I plead the Blood of Jesus Christ over everything that concerns me today and forever.

By the Blood of Jesus Christ, I declare my victory over witchcraft, the spirit of Jezebel, and the devil himself, in Jesus name.

Heavenly Father, according to Your WORD, Let the walls and defenses of witchcraft against my life, my destiny, and my family be torn down and let every form of witchcraft against me be put to an end from this day and forever, in Jesus name.

O Lord, frustrate every witch, every wizard, every Jezebel, and every fortune teller against my life and family.

Let disgrace and shame become the lot of witches and wizards working against my life at any level from today onwards, in Jesus name.

Father in the name of Jesus Christ, I speak into the spirit world this day; I speak into the air; I speak into the land, and I speak into the sea. I speak into the four corners of the earth, and I speak into all spiritual kingdoms that are not seen by man.

I command fire from heaven to scatter every evil gathering of witches and wizards and wicked men and women against my life and family, every kind of meeting that has taken place or will take place ever again. I command them to scatter and be destroyed by fire from heaven, in Jesus name.

I break the power of witchcraft's deception, seduction, sorcery, domination, and intimidation over my life and family, in the name of Jesus Christ.

Every seat of witchcraft in my household, be destroyed by fire right now, in Jesus name.

O Lord, let every evil instrument of witchcraft deposited in my life and family catch fire right now and be destroyed.

It is written, "Every plant that God has not planted shall be rooted out" (Matthew 15:13).

I, therefore, command every evil seed in the form of strife, quarrels, disfavor, hatred, nightmares, illnesses, disappointments, and confusions planted in my life, against my life or in my family to be uprooted by fire this moment, in Jesus name.

May whatever I have eaten out of ignorance that was a connecting point between me and witchcraft manipulation be exposed and purged out of my life and family, and destroyed by fire, in Jesus name.

I reverse all witchcraft curses, covenants, spells, and incantations against my life and family this day.

I command God's blessings of love, favor, prosperity, and abundant life to replace every evil pronouncement and decree made against my family and me by witches, wizards, and people with the spirit of Jezebel, in Jesus name.

O Lord, because the hearts of men and kings are in Your Hands and You turn them wherever pleases YOU (Proverbs 21:1); I ask that from today, YOU turn the hearts of men and women to work for my favor and progress wherever I go.

Whatever I have lost, and whatever have been denied me in life as a result of the activities of witchcraft and wicked forces of darkness or evil men, I claim a seven-fold restoration this day, in Jesus name.

O Lord, I present my spouse, family, and children before You this year. I present our career, our ministry, our business, our community and our neighbors before You. I break the bonds of darkness, witchcraft, and Jezebel over us all, and I set us free to serve God, in Jesus name.

Against Charismatic Witchcraft

Most Gracious Father, I ask You to forgive me, in any way I have surrendered myself to men and women who come in Your name but are using evil powers. I believe I didn't listen enough to You, which was why I submitted to their tricks.

I believe You tried to warn me, but perhaps I placed my own needs far above Your instruction.

Heavenly Father, just like the prodigal son, I come back and ask for forgiveness. For the sake of the shed Blood of Jesus Christ, please forgive me, in Jesus name.

Father, I stand in authority in the name of Jesus Christ and bind every demon released into my life, family, home, marriage, and business, by wolves in sheep's clothing – false men and women of God. I command these demons to pack their loads and leave my life right now and go back into the abyss, in Jesus name.

I break every tie and spiritual connection between me and demons projected through demonic men and women who pretend to be from God.

I command every evil deposit in my life and family by false preachers and teachers to be destroyed by fire this day, in Jesus name.

O Lord, from now onwards, correct every wrong mindset I have accepted from false, pretentious preachers, and teachers that are working against my life and destiny.

I declare total restoration and healing of any part of my life that have been tampered with by my ignorant submission to these appealing deceivers in Jesus name.

I decree today that there shall be no more witchcraft against my life, against my home, against my marriage, against my finances, and against my destiny, in Jesus name.

Lord, I thank You for putting an end to the power of witchcraft against me and blessing me with favor and peace roundabout.

May You alone be glorified and praised forever and ever, in Jesus name.

Day 12: **No More Strongholds**

Culled from the book, <u>Deliverance by Fire</u>

For the weapons of our warfare are not carnal but mighty in God to pull down of strongholds, ₅ casting down arguments and every high thing that exalts itself against the knowledge of God, bringing every thought into captivity to the obedience of Christ, ₆and being ready to punish all disobedience when your obedience is fulfilled.- **2 Corinthians 10:4-6**

Strongholds are lies that we have accepted as truths. I call them Satan's propaganda that we unconsciously accept and hold against God's Words. Unfortunately, they are just lies that have been repeatedly told to us over and over, such that we now vigorously defend them unknowingly.

In today's reading, Paul describes strongholds as arguments, pretensions, or thoughts that set themselves contrary to the knowledge of God. Any principles, theories, views, or beliefs ingrained in our thinking that are different to the truth as written in Scripture are strongholds of the Enemy that stand in the way of our knowing God and making Him known. Thus they draw us back in our walk with the Lord and our prayer and worship lives.

Here are a few examples of strongholds:

- I will never get out of debt

- I will never be free from this addiction

- I am no good; I am worthless

- I won't find love after all

- My husband is hopeless. He'll never be saved.

- I'm just a fleshy person. I'll never be free from lust.

- I'll always struggle to make ends meet.

- I always have this sickness. It's a part of me.

- I'll probably never get married

Each of these arguments reflects interpretations rooted in the mind that are contrary to God's will. These deceptions which form mental strongholds can come from a wide range of sources, including our environment, failed relationships, friendships, parents, news, medical diagnosis, experiences of failure and pain in the past, or demons. Letting these lies control us can lead to living a defeated life.

Strongholds can also be physical. Physical strongholds are negative habits and attitudes in us that are continually struggling with our knowing God. The more we struggle with these habits, the more the enemy builds further limitations against our lives.

For instance, you may be praying to lose weight, while you're still tied to overeating. In this instance, overeating becomes a stronghold fighting against God's health plan for your life.

You may be praying for financial deliverance and breakthrough while you're still tied to impulse buying, ignoring your bills, careless spending, always expecting financial miracles instead of looking for work, and spending more than you earn. In this case, your negative financial habits are strongholds that must be dealt with for you to experience God's financial breakthrough.

Today, we're going to take time to speak into our lives and command every mental or physical stronghold that gives the devil a leeway to build a blockade over our lives and destiny to be destroyed. We are going to receive total empowerment to break free from these mental deceptions and habits that are inimical to our spiritual and physical progress.

PRAYERS

Father in heaven, by Your mercies, I come to present my life, my thoughts, and my body to You this year as a living sacrifice. Make me holy and acceptable to Your service, in Jesus name.

O Lord, I hand over my thoughts and dedicate my mind, imaginations, and attitudes to You. I ask that You uproot out of my life every inner argument, every emotional disagreement, and unbelief contesting Your Word in my life.

I arrest all negative thoughts in me, resisting the move of the Holy Spirit. I command these thoughts to wither by fire in the name of Jesus Christ.

Father, I present these strongholds to You today. I bring them under Thy feet that I may find mercy and help for freedom from these binding issues. O Lord, here are the strongholds that I see in my life

....

Mention specific strongholds in your life that needs to leave

Father, deliver me from these strongholds, in Jesus name.

May every false god contesting for worship in my life cease to exist today, in Jesus name.

Every Idol in my life challenging Lordship with You, Lord Jesus Christ, I overthrow them today by fire in the name of Jesus.

I command the idols of mammon, greed, lust, pornography, anger, bitterness **(mention other idols)** over my life to die by fire today in the name of Jesus Christ.

By the priceless Blood of Jesus Christ, I severe myself from every mental stronghold binding me to the devil and limiting the blessings of God in my life. I declare my thoughts, imaginations, brain, and meditations sanctified by the Blood of Jesus Christ, in Jesus name.

I speak to every physical stronghold of bad habit in my life to end today, in the name of Jesus.

I squeeze the life out of the powers responsible for these negative habits in my life. I command them to seize to exist. And I claim my freedom in Jesus name.

You demons pushing me to sin and live against the knowledge and will of God for my life, I bind you all *today and send you all into the abyss. Remain there and come back no more into my life in Jesus name.*

No demon has a legal right over my life anymore, for my life is hid in Christ and Christ in God. The life I live now is not mine, but Christ's. So I declare that I will live every day of my life for the Glory of God, in Jesus name.

I command fire from heaven to destroy every root of sin and ungodly habit in my life, causing a barrier between me and the power of God, in Jesus name.

O Lord, plant in me an everlasting hatred for lust, anger, bitterness, alcoholism, smoking, overeating (gluttony), and any other detrimental lifestyle hitherto warring against me and frustrating my spiritual growth, in Jesus name.

O Lord, may whatever evil consequence in my life, resulting from my attitude, past mistakes, or addictions to negative thoughts, words, and habits, seize today. Whatever curses and obstacles that my wrong thoughts, words, behaviors, associations, and friendships have brought upon my life, let them be destroyed today in the name of Jesus Christ.

O Lord, surround me with the right people – surround me with people who will challenge me towards a Godly and excellent life – from today.

I commit myself never to walk in the counsel of the ungodly, nor stand in the way of sinners, nor dine with mockers. I commit myself to delight in the Word of God and fellowship.

I shall henceforth depend on God's Word day and night, and its power shall work in me, always, to bear the right fruits.

I am like a tree planted by the side of the river. My strength shall not fail. From season to season, I shall bear fruit... in Jesus Mighty name.

Amen.

Day 13: **Advance Forgiveness**

₂₁David came to the two hundred men who were so exhausted that they could not follow him and had been left at the brook Besor with the provisions. They went out to meet David and the people with him, and when he approached the people, he greeted them.

₂₂Then all the wicked and worthless men among those who went with David said, "Because they did not go with us, we will give them none of the spoil that we have recovered, except that each man may take his wife and children away and leave."

₂₃David said, "You must not do so, my brothers, with what the Lord has given us. He has kept us safe and has handed over to us the band of Amalekites that came against us.

₂₄And who will listen to you regarding this matter? For as is the share of him who goes down into the battle, so shall his share be who stays by the provisions and supplies; they shall share alike."

This is an exciting story. David refused to pay evil with evil. He forgave and distributed the spoils equally to everyone.

These men had wanted to stone him earlier on for an offense he did not commit. He encouraged himself in the Lord, mustered the strength to chase the enemy. The men did not join him in the chase. But when God gave him victory, he still thought to share the spoils with them.

That's the key to consistently winning with God:

> *"You must forgive offenses, as quickly as possible, and move on, to fully stay in the will and blessings of God for your life."*

The Bible says: *"Whenever you stand to pray, forgive if you have anything against anyone so that your Father who is in heaven will also forgive you your transgressions. But if you do not forgive, neither will your Father who is in heaven forgive your transgressions."* (Mark 11:25-26)

Many times it won't be easy to practice forgiveness especially when we begin to consider the scale of the offenses that took place. However, if we're going to stay in the will of God, and manifest His blessings for our lives, we must embrace forgiveness. From time to time, we must come before God and prayerfully forgive all offenses and let God take control.

In fact, we need to learn to forgive in advance. By that I mean we need to choose to forgive offenses even before they are committed against us.

When we chose to walk in forgiveness this way, we are simply accepting the fallibility of people and not trusting too much. We are giving room never to allow people's negative interpretations and reactions towards us to choke the love of God in our lives. We're telling ourselves, say, *"Hey, come what may, there's no room for anger, bitterness, depression, and other negative feelings in my life this year."*

Someone said, "Unforgiveness is like drinking poison yourself and waiting for the other person to die."

And you know what, she's right.

"Unforgiveness does more harm to us than the offenders. It is like serving a prison term for the offense of someone else. That's why I encourage people to practice advance forgiveness."

As the year progresses, mistakes will be made, and offenses will come. But resolving to move on ahead of time will energize you to overcome the urge to fight back when these attacks occur.

There is nothing unforgivable, and there are no pains that our God cannot help you overcome. Sit down, pray, and say, "Lord, help me to do this. Help me to forgive."

The Bible says, *"Bear with each other and forgive whatever grievances you may have against one another. Forgive as the Lord forgave you"* (Colossians 3:13).

PRAYERS

Heavenly Father, I honor and bless You this day and forever.

With all my soul and all that is within me, I bless Your holy Name. It is You, Father, who crowns me with love and tender mercies, and You fill my life with good things.

I give thanks to You and proclaim your greatness.

Thank You, Father, for loving me, forgiving me, and saving me. Thank You for being patient with me. Your compassion towards me is unfailing, and Your mercies are new every morning. Lord, Your faithfulness is great towards me.

Receive my praise forever and ever, in Jesus name

O Lord, please forgive me for not being forgiving.

Forgive me for seeking revenge against people who have offended me.

Forgive me for bearing grudges, and for not walking in love completely.

Forgive me for gossiping, lying, and for rehearsing in my mind what was said or done to me.

Lord, remind me of everyone I need to forgive and help me to forgive.

Heavenly Father, I ask for forgiveness of all the damaging and hurtful words I have spoken about myself in the past.

I do not want to continue to abuse, deride, and debase myself in such ways again.

Renew my thoughts and help me to understand and appreciate that You have made me in Your image and likeness.

Empower my attitudes and habits henceforth, so that I use my tongue to speak faith, hope, love, and favor upon my life. In Jesus' name.

Father, Your Word tells me that if I forgive those who have sinned against me, then You will forgive me. But, if I refuse to forgive others, You will not forgive me too.

Today I choose to forgive.

Father, I declare that I will be patient with people and forgive those who have offended me.

And I forgive .... for ...., and I release them and let it go.

In Jesus name

Holy Spirit, help all of me to forgive people who have hurt me.

Heal my emotions that have been injured and teach me how to love unconditionally.

Continue to extend Your love and mercy toward me. Please remind me daily to use Your power living on the inside of me, which helps me in all things.

Help me to forget the past so that I can move forward to the future as I press toward the mark of my higher calling in Christ Jesus, in Jesus name.

Holy Spirit, please empower me all through this year and beyond to walk in love, always forgiving and looking up to You in all things, in Jesus name.

I command every root of anger, bitterness, and unforgiveness in my life to be destroyed this moment in Jesus name.

O Lord, I pray this day, restore to me whatever has been damaged in my life and family as a result of bitterness, anger, and unforgiveness in the past, in Jesus name.

Heal me O Lord, and I shall be healed. Restore me, O Lord, and I shall be restored. Empower me, Lord, and I shall be empowered.

All-round victory, restoration, and breakthrough is my portion this year, in Jesus name.

Day 14: **Awaken Your Gifts**

"For we are God's handiwork, created in Christ Jesus to do good works, which God prepared in advance for us to do." - Eph 2:10 (NIV)

If we will arise and shine this year, then we must prayerfully awaken our gifts. God blessed us all with powerful gifts and talents, which if used, will empower us to excel in the world irrespective of the darkness in it. That is why our prayer today is focused on awakening God's gifts, skills, and talents in our lives.

Before we proceed, make these declarations:

- I am God's creation

- I am fearfully and wonderfully made

- I am created in Christ Jesus

- I am created to do good works

- I am blessed with unique gifts and skills

- God will use my gifts and abilities for his glory, in Jesus name.

I believe that if every Christian functioned effectively in their gifts, the world would be so afraid of us because of how we excel. Unfortunately, we seem to be stuck with struggling to get our daily needs met that we don't even have time to question the unique gifts and skills God gave us. We end up like the guy in Jesus' parable who went and hid his talent out of fear.

> "It's also like a man going off on an extended trip. He called his servants together and delegated responsibilities. To one, he gave five thousand dollars, to another two thousand, to a third one thousand, depending on their abilities. Then he left. Right off, the first servant went to work and doubled his master's investment. The second did the same. But the man with the single thousand dug a hole and carefully buried his master's money." - **Matthew 25:14-18** (MSG)

The Message Bible translated the word **talents** into money here because these talents equal to money. If we recognize our gifts, skills, and talents, they will not just advance the kingdom; they will also advance our lives economically. That is why I believe that this call to consecration is not complete without us praying to wake up our gifts, skills, and callings.

FOR MEDITATION

Matthew 25: 14-30 (MSG) - It's also like a man going off on an extended trip. He called his servants together and delegated responsibilities. To one, he gave five thousand dollars to another two thousand, to a third one thousand, depending on their abilities. Then he left. Right off, the first servant went to work and doubled his master's investment. The second did the same. But the man with the single thousand dug a hole and ....

1 Peter 4:10-11 (ESV) - 10 As each has received a gift, use it to serve one another, as good stewards of God's varied grace: 11 whoever speaks, as one who speaks oracles of God; whoever serves, as one who serves by the strength that God supplies—in order that in everything God may be glorified through Jesus Christ. To him belong glory and dominion forever and ever. Amen.

Romans 12:1-21 (ESV) - I appeal to you, therefore, brothers, by the mercies of God, to present your bodies as a living sacrifice, holy and acceptable to God, which is your spiritual worship. Do not be conformed to this world, but be transformed by the renewal of your mind, that by testing you may discern what the will of God is, what is good and acceptable and perfect.

PRAYERS

Heavenly Father, give me the wisdom to recognize the gifts and talents you have blessed me with, in Jesus name.

O Lord, grant me opportunities and open doors this year to put my gifts into profitable use, for Your kingdom advancement, and for my betterment, in Jesus name.

May all my buried and undiscovered gifts begin to manifest today by the fire of the Holy Spirit, in the name of Jesus Christ.

O Lord, I dedicate and consecrate my gifts, skills, and talents to You. I recognize that You are the creator and giver of all good gifts. May I only become what You have designed me to become, and may my gifts and skills glorify Your name on this earth, in Jesus name.

This year, I will bear fruits that bring glory to Jesus Christ, for *God has called me to bear fruits. So I will not be barren. My life will be fruitful, both spiritually and physically. Through my gifts and skills, God's kingdom will go forward. Through my gifts, my generation will be blessed, in Jesus name.*

In the name of Jesus Christ, I decree that I will not leave this world without making use of all the gifts and callings that God has given to me. This world will be blessed through my life, gifts, and talents, in Jesus name.

May *every attack on my gifts and skills, designed to frustrate and keep me unfulfilled cease today, in the name of Jesus Christ.*

I command all my gifts, skills, and talents to wake up from this day forward, and begin to speak loudly, in Jesus name.

I command every spirit of fear, indiscipline, and laziness, projected to keep my gifts and skills from speaking out, to lose their grips on me from this day forward. I set myself free from all forms of limitations against my gifts and abilities, and decree that I will henceforth excel in what God has empowered me to do and become, in Jesus name.

Today, and onwards, I receive grace, wisdom, and strength to labor on the gifts and talents that I have received from God, in Jesus name

Day 15: **Pray For the Land**

"I urge, then, first of all, that petitions, prayers, intercession, and thanksgiving be made for all people— 2 for kings and all those in authority, that we may live peaceful and quiet lives in all godliness and holiness." - **1 Timothy 2:1-2**

Today, let's pray for our nation, our state, and our various communities. We may not have the physical openings to look at our politicians and reps in the face and rebuke them, but our prayers can go a long way in helping to shape our land.

The Bible says, *"If my people, which are called by my name, shall humble themselves, and pray, and seek my face, and turn from their wicked ways; then will I hear from heaven, and will forgive their sin, and will heal their land"* (2 Chronicles 7:14).

Our prayers can provoke divine intervention in our political and economic landscape. And until there is a supernatural intervention in the land, there will be no breakthrough for the Church.

> Pray for peace in Jerusalem. May all who love this city prosper. - Psalm 122:6 (NLT)

Our country, our states, our cities, and our neighborhoods represent our Jerusalem today. If there is no peace in the land, we will be affected in some ways. If the economy is horrible, we may be affected at some point.

Thankfully, God says that if we sincerely pray for the land, He will heal the land, give us breakthrough and cause us to possess the land spiritually, and excel in it.

Yes, there are times I feel it's waste praying for my country, especially when physical events in politics does not reflect our prayers. I find myself struggling, wondering why politicians are able to deceive us, play on our intelligence, loot our shared heritage and walk boldly away without any punishment.

I'm sure I'm not the only Christian who struggles many times with the idea of praying for our nations and communities. But we can encourage ourselves knowing that God is working things out for our good even when physical events don't say so.

Our land desperately needs the life-giving renewal and redemption that flow from Christ's life, death and resurrection.

PRAYERS

For Our Host Community & Country

Father, in the name of Jesus Christ, I thank You for making me a part of this community and neighborhood. Thank You for making me a citizen of this country.

It was not by accident that You brought me to live and work in this place. So I praise Your name forever and ever, in Jesus name.

O Lord, according to Your Word, my light will continue to shine in this land and will never be hidden. I will be an example of righteousness and the blessings of God in this community, in Jesus name.

I decree that the lamp of my salvation will never be put out in this land. Whatever is working to put out my lamp in this community, O Lord, I frustrate them today, in Jesus name.

Any evil spirit claiming ownership of this land and working against God's people and the Gospel, I overthrow you this day and cast you into the abyss in Jesus name.

I break all forms of resistance against the prayers of believers in this land.

Let the warring angels of heaven be released this day and oppose all spiritual oppositions causing blockades for the prayers of believers in this community and neighborhood and begin to hasten answers to all prayers, in Jesus name.

I raise the banner of victory over this city and declare that Jesus Christ is the LORD and ruler of this land, in Jesus name.

By the Blood of Jesus Christ, I command all demonic prison doors holding men and women from coming to the knowledge of Christ to be destroyed right now, in Jesus name.

Holy Spirit, begin to move in this community and convict men, women, and children to accept Jesus Christ as their LORD and Savior, in Jesus name.

Heavenly Father, I pray for the peace and prosperity of this neighborhood and this nation.

May the inhabitants of this neighborhood and community come to the knowledge of Jesus Christ.

May they prosper and may peace be within the walls of this land, in Jesus name.

O LORD, may the Light of the Gospel shine deep in this land and may darkness be leveled completely, in Jesus name.

Every witchcraft and python spirit afflicting this neighborhood and community, I bind and cast you into the abyss this day, in Jesus name.

I tear down all strongholds in and surrounding this town/city. I bind and rebuke them, and command them to be destroyed today, in Jesus name.

Father Lord, I lift up my country before thee. I pray that Your Love will prevail in all the land, and Your knowledge will reign supreme over all flesh, in Jesus name.

I break every curse that has been put against this community, its inhabitants, the county, and the state of [name] by persons living or dead, in Jesus name.

I claim victory over the city and town of [name], I claim victory over the county of [name], I claim victory over the state of [name], and all inhabitants thereof, in the name of Jesus Christ.

I plead the blood of Jesus Christ over this land, and I station angels in all the four corners of this community.

I declare that the will of God will be done in this land, in Jesus name.

I renounce the works of Baal in this land. And I expel the spirit of Baal and false worship in the state and this nation. May all the prophets of Baal in this land be exposed this day, in Jesus name.

I pull down every stronghold, and every altar of Baal and Ashtaroth established in any part of this neighborhood, community, state and the nation. I command all the operations of Baal and the prophets to seize in Jesus name.

You spirits of mammon and Molech that have invaded the Church, I bind you all this day, and I command all your operations in the Church to seize this moment, in Jesus name.

O Lord, intervene in Your church. Expose all the evil operators that are causing reproach to the name of Christ. Send us revival and glorify the name of Your Son, Jesus Christ, in Jesus name.

Thank You Heavenly Father for answered prayers, in Jesus name

Day 16: **Your Words and Meditations**

₁₃Keep back thy servant also from presumptuous sins; let them not have dominion over me: then shall I be upright, and I shall be innocent from the great transgression.

₁₄Let the words of my mouth, and the meditation of my heart, be acceptable in thy sight, O Lord, my strength, and my redeemer. - Psalm 19:13-14

In these scriptures, the Psalmist prayed two important prayers that we ought to pray as well. First, he prays that God will prevent him from committing presumptuous sins; that these presumptuous sins would not have dominion over him.

What are presumptuous sins?

Presumptuous here means arrogant, proud, overconfident, egotistical, and overbold. The Psalmist is praying that his successes would not make him be too full of himself that he would not recognize His daily need of God anymore.

How often do we let our past victories, successes, and testimonies make us think that we have mastered God and that we understand Him better than others. This is a line we don't want to cross in our faith journey: *to think that we are better than other Christians because God has used or is using us to accomplish great things.* It is a sin of the heart; it can make one arrogant, un-teachable, and overconfident on their ability. Like David, we must pray that God will keep us away from this sin and not let it control us.

Secondly, David also prayed that the words of his mouth and the meditation of his heart would be acceptable unto the Lord, his strength. Why do we need to pray this prayer with unswerving focus as well? Because our meditations and words influence every other aspect of our lives.

Your thoughts influence your words and your words control your destiny.

To arise and shine this year, one of the areas we must work on is on our thoughts and spoken words. We may spend 100 days praying and fasting, but if our thoughts and spoken words are not renewed, are continually negative and filthy, our answers will hardly manifest.

Every one of us has spiritual authority over our lives and destinies, and one of the ways we exercise this authority is through our thoughts and spoken words. If you regularly think and speak faith-filled words, you create empowerment, peace, blessings, and prosperity as returns. But if you continuously think and speak fear-filled words, you create weakness, crisis, curses, and poverty as returns.

The Bible says:

> "Do not be conformed to this world, but be transformed by the renewing of your mind, that you may prove what is that good and acceptable and perfect will of God" (Romans 12:2).

It is very important to surrender your thoughts and words to the Lord this year and learn to bless continually. You may face challenges, but your thoughts and words must bless and continually call forth into existence things that you desire to manifest in your life.

Finally, brethren, whatever things are true, whatever things are noble, whatever things are just, whatever things are pure, whatever things are lovely, whatever things are of good report, if there is any virtue and if there is anything praiseworthy—meditate on these things – Philippians 4:8

CALLING FORTH INTO EXISTENCE...

God changed Abram's name to Abraham to teach him and us one secret about Him: He does not look at our negative situations but on His plans for our lives.

Abram means high father, while Abraham means father of a multitude.

In Abraham's eyes, he was a man who needed a son to keep his lineage going. But in God's eyes, Abraham was the father of many nations. So to get Abraham on the same page with Him, God changed his name from Abram to Abraham.

> As it is written, I have made thee a father of many nations,) before him whom he believed, even God, who quickeneth the dead, and calleth those things which be not as though they were. - Romans 4:17

If God were to appear to you physically today, He will not address you as:

- *"Hey! You poor, sick, helpless, tormented fellow. You have no hope."*

He'll likely say to you:

- *"You great man/woman of God...*
- *"You mighty man/woman of valor...*
- *"You deliverer of the people*
- *"You are highly favored...*
- *"You are healed...*

God does not call you by your circumstances but by His Word for your life. In the same way, learn to quit calling yourself by your circumstances but by God's Word for your life. This is very important if we must arise and shine this year.

Today's, come before God in high praise and decree His words over your life and family. Call forth His plans and promises for your life into existence.

Are you in debt? Do you need a breakthrough in career and business? Come in prayer tonight and decree supernatural deliverance and advancement.

What are your earnest expectations and desires? Write them down tonight and begin to decree their existence. *"As I live,' says the Lord, 'just as you have spoken in My hearing, so I will do to you"* (Numbers 14:28).

PRAYERS AND DECLARATIONS

Precious Father, I pray today, keep me humble and teachable all the days of my life in Jesus name.

This year, Lord, keep me away from presumptuous sins and cause me to recognize my need of You every day, in Jesus name.

Father, let the words of my mouth and the meditations of my heart be acceptable unto You. Keep my mind stayed on You at all times and help me to overcome negative thoughts that come to steal, kill, and destroy my life, in Jesus name.

Father, Lord, I ask for forgiveness from all negative words, evil statements, fearful and faithless pronouncements that have ever proceeded out of my mouth, which is now creating barriers and spiritual judgments for me.

By the blood of Jesus Christ, I receive total healing and deliverance from all negative consequences of my words, in Jesus name.

In the name of Jesus Christ, I receive grace to keep my tongue from speaking evil and my lips from telling lies this year (Psalm 34:13).

O Lord, set a guard over my mouth and keep watch over the door of my lips. This year, may my tongue only give wise advise, and bring healing to myself and to all who listen to me, in the name of Jesus Christ.

Henceforth, I acknowledge myself as a messenger of grace, encouragement, and healing this year. May my words reflect these virtues in Jesus name (Proverbs 16:24).

O Lord, from this day forward, help me to see myself in your perspective and not from the standpoint of the world or the viewpoint of my circumstances.

I command myself not to be hasty with words this year.

Holy Spirit, I ask that You always remind me when I am about to fall short of this commitment, and enable me to choose that which pleases the Lord always, in Jesus name

Today, I decree that light will shine on my ways all through this year. I decree that people's opinions and experts' analyses will not control my thoughts and judgments about my life from now onwards, in Jesus name.

I am a child of God, created in the image of God, to have dominion, replenish, and be fruitful. That is exactly what I'm having all through this year.

As the heavens are far above the earth, so are God's ways far above my ways.

I decree today that everything that was planned for my hurt is turning for my testimony from this day forward, in Jesus name.

Go ahead and begin to make specific Bible-based declarations and call forth your expectations into existence this year, in Jesus name.

Thank You, Lord, for the victory that I have from this day forward, in Jesus name.

Day 17: **The Fruit of the Spirit**

₂₂But the fruit of the Spirit is love, joy, peace, longsuffering, kindness, goodness, faithfulness, ₂₃gentleness, self-control. Against such there is no law. - Galatians 5:22-23

The fruit of the Holy Spirit is God's characteristics produced in the life of the believer by the Holy Spirit. The Scripture lists them as love, joy, peace, longsuffering, kindness, goodness, faithfulness, gentleness, and self-control. As humans, these qualities are not always easy to grow without help. But with the Holy Spirit in us, we can manifest them every day because, in truth, we are not the ones bearing the fruit; it is the Holy Spirit in us who bears the fruit.

A Christian can rely on the Holy Spirit to love even in the most challenging moments, be joyful even when there is no reason to, have peace in troublous times, be patient when there is no need to, and exercise self-control. Why?

Because the Holy Spirit bears these fruit in our lives, not we trying to work out some great qualities.

However, just as natural fruit needs time to nurture, the fruit of the Holy Spirit will not mature in our lives overnight. As every successful gardener must fight against weeds to enjoy the fruit they desire, we must continually work to get rid of the "weeds" of our old self that always strives to gag the work of the Holy Spirit in us.

- You can love no matter the circumstances

- You can be joyful even when things seems messed up

- You can have peace even in very troublous times

- You can be tolerant, forgiving, and patient even with the most venomous person on earth

- You can be good, faithful, and gentle, both with yourself and with others notwithstanding all the unfavorable conditions and reasons not to be

- You can have self-control so that you're free from every harmful addiction

The Holy Spirit is the Seed that produces these qualities. He is already in us. All we need to do is let Him, depend on Him to work out these fruit in our lives. As we give Him more control of our lives every day, He begins to do in us and through us what only He can do – shaping us and molding us to look like Jesus.

> [17] Now the Lord is the Spirit; and where the Spirit of the Lord is, there is liberty. [18] But we all, with unveiled face, beholding as in a mirror the glory of the Lord, are being transformed into the same image from glory to glory, just as by the Spirit of the Lord. - 2 Corinthians 3:17-18

PRAYER

For The Fruit of the Holy Spirit

Heavenly Father,

Thank You for engrafting me in Christ Jesus by the Holy Spirit as a branch. You designed me to bear fruit of righteousness, love, peace, joy, gentleness, self-control, goodness, patience, and kindness.

O Lord, I desire to bear these fruits in my life henceforth,

Holy Spirit, I desire to remain rooted in Christ, bearing fruit that leads others to the light of God's love. I desire to walk in LOVE, forgiving others at all times, and gifting God's blessings on my life with others, just as God Loved and gave Jesus to die for us.

I desire, every day, to walk in joy, peace, gentleness, self-control, goodness, patience, and kindness so that I will be an example that brings others to Christ. Help me, empower me, and teach me to bear Your fruit every day in Jesus name.

Holy Spirit, I desire to walk in peace with myself and with others as a child of God.

I desire to walk in patience, for faith makes no haste.

I desire to walk in kindness, thoughtfulness, and compassion for others, just as Christ was compassionate at all times.

Provide me with daily assistance to bear these fruits of peace, patience, and kindness in abundance, so that

Jesus will be glorified in my life every day, in Jesus name.

Holy Spirit, I desire to bear the fruit of Goodness, so that I may lead others to Jesus Christ.

I desire to be faithful at all times with whatever God blesses me with so that I may stand before God in the end and receive the rewards of faithfulness.

I desire to be gentle with myself and others, in thoughts, words, and actions, so that I may be an instrument of encouragement and uplifting to others and not discouragement.

I desire to walk in Self-control in food, dressing, and in everything so that I could win the race set before me and not be a cast away after preaching to others.

I call upon You to empower me every day to bear these fruits as I live, serve God, and relate with others, in Jesus name, I pray. Amen.

Day 18: **I Shall Not Die**

"With long life will I satisfy him, and shew him my salvation." - Psalms 91:16

God wants us to live a long, healthy life. Premature death is not part of His agenda for His children. However, long life is a promise that comes with some conditions. In Psalm 34:12-14, the requirements include:

- keeping the tongue from negativity,

- not speaking lies,

- departing from evil,

- doing good,

- and seeking and pursuing peace.

In Psalm 91:14-16, a long life comes with a condition of loving the Lord. And in Proverbs 3:1-2, the promise of long life comes with obeying the laws and commandments of God.

The good thing is that these commands are not grievous. The Holy Spirit is given to us to help us walk with God and obey His commandments.

So, today, let us remind God His promise to sustain us, preserve our lives, and take authority against premature death.

You shall not die but live to declare the goodness of God.

PRAYERS AND DECLARATIONS

Father Lord, I thank You LORD for the promise of long life to those who obey you. I praise and magnify Your name, this day, and forever, in Jesus name.

Lord, I commit the totality of my life into Your hand this year and beyond; help me by the Holy Spirit to walk in Your ways and to keep Your commandments.

Lord, engrave Your fear in my heart every day, for it is written that the fear of the LORD prolongs days (Prov. 10:27).

Holy Spirit, empower me daily to obey and serve God, so that I may spend my days in prosperity and my years in joy and strength (Job 36:11).

Plant the laws and commandments of God in my heart and help me never to forget them, and may they lengthen my days and cause me to dwell in peace and security, in Jesus name (Proverbs 3:1-2).

I declare this day, according to the Word of God, that I shall not die but live and continue to proclaim the goodness of God, in Jesus name (Psalm 118:17).

This year, no member of my family shall die in Jesus name.

I decree that we shall fulfill the number of our years. We shall live to eat the fruit of our labor, for we shall not labor for another to enjoy, in Jesus name (Isaiah 65:23).

Today, I rebuke the spirit of death and cast it into the abyss.

I decree that there shall be no mourning and shedding of tears in my family this year, in Jesus name.

All through this year, O LORD, I cover myself and my family with the precious Blood of Jesus Christ. May the Blood of Jesus Christ continue to speak in our favor, in Jesus name.

The LORD God Almighty shall satisfy us with long life, and under His wings shall we find refuge, in Jesus name.

Amen

Day 19: **How to Live a Blessed Life**

₃₀ Then Jesus answered and said: "A certain man went down from Jerusalem to Jericho, and fell among thieves, who stripped him of his clothing, wounded him, and departed, leaving him half dead.

₃₁ Now by chance a certain priest came down that road. And when he saw him, he passed by on the other side. ₃₂ Likewise a Levite, when he arrived at the place, came and looked, and passed by on the other side.

₃₃ But a certain Samaritan, as he journeyed, came where he was. And when he saw him, he had compassion. ₃₄ So he went to him and bandaged his wounds, pouring on oil and wine; and he set him on his own animal, brought him to an inn, and took care of him.

₃₅ On the next day, when he departed, he took out two denarii, gave them to the innkeeper, and said to him, 'Take care of him; and whatever more you spend, when I come again, I will repay you.' ₃₆ So which of these three do you think was neighbor to him who fell among the thieves?"

₃₇ And he said, "He who showed mercy on him." Then Jesus said to him, "Go and do likewise." – Luke 10:30-37

The parable of the Good Samaritan is one of the most famous parables of Christ. Today, we use the word, "Good Samaritan," when we want to talk about those who go out of their way to help others at their own expense. Let's remind ourselves what this Parable is and what Jesus taught with it.

While Jesus was ministering one day, an expert in the laws of Moses stood up and asked Him, saying, "Teacher, what shall I do to inherit eternal life?"

This lawyer knew the letters of the law and wanted to do a public knowledge contest with Christ, probably to find what to use against him. He wasn't asking because he wanted to know, he was asking only to prove his smartness and get Christ ensnared with his sayings.

Jesus replied by asking him, "What is written in the law? What is your reading of it?" The expert answered and said, "'You shall love the Lord your God with all your heart, with all your soul, with all your strength, and with all your mind,' and 'your neighbor as yourself.' " Then Jesus replied, "You have answered rightly; do this, and you will live."

But he, wanting to justify himself, said to Jesus, "And who is my neighbor?"

To answer the question of whom a person's neighbor is, Jesus told this parable, and it shut the lawyer up. Jesus asked the expert, and by extension us, to follow the example of the Samaritan.

WHO WERE THE SAMARITANS?

The Samaritans were regarded as sinners and discriminated against by the Jews. They were originally from the tribes of Ephraim and Manasseh. But when Israel was divided into North and Southern Kingdoms, they were captured by the Assyrians and intermarried with them, evolving into what became as Samaria. So a Samaritan of Jesus' day was half-Jew and half Gentile.

The Jews believed that the Samaritans had fallen out of the right path and were idol worshippers. Their relationship was so bad that the Jews would never walk in Samaria but would go far out of their way, even if their journey was longer, so that they would avoid entering Samaria.

This is precisely why Jesus cited the Samaritan in this parable because he would be the most unlikely ever to help a Jew in trouble. The Samaritans also hated the Jews in the same measure the Jews hated them.

LEARN FROM THE GOOD SAMARITAN

Even though Jesus gave this parable to show the expert who his neighbor was, there are fascinating lessons for us in the story.

#1. Lend a Helping Hand: The man robbed by thieves represents others who are robbed in life of one thing or the other. Our society is filled with hundreds of them. The religion that God our Father accepts as pure and faultless is to look after the helpless, the orphans, the widows, the abused, and those in distress, and to keep oneself from being polluted by the world. We all have something we can do to relieve others of their pains.

#2. Say No to Racism and Tribalism: The Samaritan did not consider that there was an ethnic hatred between them and the Jews. He saw a human who needed help and offered to support. He risked an eventual attack from other Samaritans for what he did, but that didn't stop him. As long as he was concerned, this was a human.

We must understand that we are first and foremost humans, before color, tribe, and nationality.

> ### *When dealing with people, forget about their tribes, color, or race.*

Deal with them as humans. Help them as humans. That is how to be a good Samaritan.

#3. It May Cost Something: Helping others can cost you time and money. The Good Samaritan couldn't continue his journey for that day. Helping that fellow cost his time and money. But he was okay with that. He must have thought that "One person genuinely saved from distress is worth every time and penny."

Helping others will cost us time and resources. But this is a call we must all accept to live a happy and fulfilled life. Don't count the cost; count the blessings.

#4. God Can Use a Samaritan: In every aspect, this Samaritan beat all the expectation of the Jews about Samaritans. My experience in life has taught me that God can use people that we least expect. So don't let other people's views and interpretations of their sects, tribes, or races influence your rejection of humanity in them. Don't give up on anybody because of the opinion of others.

LIVING THE BLESSED LIFE

God has called us to be examples, not in the way we accumulate wealth, but in the way we serve and help others. The blessed life is the life that serves and lightens the burdens of others, not the one with the greatest possessions.

Jesus said in Matthew 5:13-16 (MSG), "Let me tell you why you are here. You're here to be salt-seasoning that brings out the God-flavors of this earth. If you lose your saltiness, how will people taste godliness? You've lost your usefulness and will end up in the garbage.

"Here's another way to put it: You're here to be light, bringing out the God-colors in the world. God is not a secret to be kept. We're going public with this, as public as a city on a hill. If I make you light-bearers, you don't think I'm going to hide you under a bucket, do you? I'm putting you on a light stand. Now that I've put you there on a hilltop, on a light stand—shine! Keep open house;

be generous with your lives. By opening up to others, you'll prompt people to open up with God, this generous Father in heaven."

If people are going to have a good view of God, then our lives are what they will use as a yardstick. The Christian life is one consecrated to God for the service of others.

Some people may never read the Bible, but they will learn from our lives who Christ is. Let us, therefore, pray today that God will give us the grace to be His witness by the way we live and serve this year.

- Choose to believe in people and their potential
- Try to see things from the perspective of other people
- Choose to create an environment of encouragement every day
- Measure your success by how much value you add to others, not by how much money you made

The Apostle Paul said, "Put yourself aside and help others get ahead. Don't be obsessed with getting your own advantage. Forget yourselves long enough to lend a helping hand" (Philippians 2:4–MSG).

PRAYERS

1. Pray that all through this year and beyond God will enable you to see people from His perspective.

2. Pray for the grace to be more forgiving this year

3. Pray for wisdom to relate with difficult people that you will encounter going forward

4. Ask God to provide you with opportunities to be a blessing to others this year.

5. Pray that your life will be an example to others.

6. Ask God to use your skills for His glory this year

7. Pray that through you, your home and the members of your family will see Christ and that His peace and glory will be revealed in your family in an exceptional way this year

8. Pray for the mind of Christ

9. Ask God for the Baptism of the spirit of humility and service.

10. Pray, say, *"O Lord, make me an instrument of encouragement to others throughout this year, in Jesus name."*

---

11. Pray, *"O Lord, empower me to focus on Christ while I serve, and not on the actions and reactions of men."*

---

12. Pray, *"Lord Jesus Christ, I want to be a better ambassador of Your kingdom this year. Uproot from me everything that is struggling with my submission and obedience."*

---

13. Pray, *O Lord, make me an instrument of Your love and mercy. Make me a witness of the Gospel both in words, good conduct, and acts of compassion. Use me to restore hope to the hopeless, peace to the confused, and healing to the sick and hurting. Empower my resources and provide me with opportunities to reach out to those in need, in Jesus name.*

---

14. Pray: *"Heavenly Father, empower my love for You to find expression in my relationship with people. Help me so that my profession of faith in Christ will be a thing of the heart marched with solid evidence of love and kindness.*

O Lord, help me and always remind me that I don't have to return people's hate with hate. Touch my heart by the Holy Spirit and inspire in me Love and kindness that glorifies You, even in difficult circumstances, in Jesus name.

All through this year, Lord, fill my heart with your endless love and lead me to share and show kindness every day of my life, in Jesus name.

Amen.

Day 20: **Victory Declarations**

Read, meditate, and declare these promises of God over yourself and your loved ones. The Word of God is powerful enough to create the realities of God in your life and destiny this year.

1. I Am God's Workmanship

"For we are God's handiwork, created in Christ Jesus to do good works, which God prepared in advance for us to do." - Ephesians 2:10

DECLARE: *I am God's design, created in Christ Jesus, reborn from above, spiritually transformed and renewed, doing good works, which God prepared for me beforehand.*

I am living the good life, which He prearranged and made ready for me.

I am walking in the Light; darkness has no place in me.

I am shinning day by day, fulfilling the plans of God for my life, in Jesus name.

2. God's Plans for Me is Peace and Hope

"For I know the plans I have for you," declares the Lord, "plans to prosper you and not to harm you, plans to give you hope and future." - Jeremiah 29:11

DECLARE: *The plan of God for my life is peace, health, and prosperity. When I pray, I have confidence that God answers my prayers.*

My future is safe and secure.

I do not need to fear and worry about life and what it brings, for God is working out everything for my good.

In Jesus name.

3. I Am a Light in the World

You are the light of the world. A city on a hill cannot be hidden. Neither do people light a lamp and put it under a basket. Instead, they set it on a lampstand, and it gives light to everyone in the house." – Matthew 5:14-15

DECLARE: *I am a light of Christ to the world. A city set on a hill that cannot be hidden.*

I am an example and a testimony to the world.

My light is shining every day, towards the perfect day.

I am excelling and winning in all that I do.

In Jesus name.

Amen

---

4. Divine Health Is Mine

Praise the Lord, my soul, and forget not all his benefits—who forgives all our sins and heals all your diseases, who redeems your life from the pit and crowns you with love and compassion." - Psalm 103:2-4

DECLARE: *"My body is God's temple.*

No sickness and disease are permitted in my body.

The death of Jesus Christ on the cross brings me total healing.

Every day, I am walking in divine health.

I have emotional peace. I have physical health, and I have spiritual strength.

I am strong in every area of my life, in Jesus name."

---

5. I am Free From Condemnation

"Therefore, there is now no condemnation for those who are in Christ Jesus, because through Christ Jesus the law of the Spirit who gives life has set you free from the law of sin and death." - Romans 8:1-2

DECLARE: *I am free from condemnation, self-pity, and self-judgment.*

I will not regret my past mistakes and failures, for all are recreated in Christ Jesus for my glory.

I am set free by the Almighty God through Christ.

I am not righteous by my own works, but by the power of the Holy Spirit.

Even though I have made grave mistakes in the past, God has forgiven me by the Blood of Jesus. No one can condemn me going forward, in Jesus name.

6. Everything Works For My Good

"And we know that in all things God works for the good of those who love him, who have been called according to his purpose." - Romans 8:28

DECLARE: *"The minds and hearts of men are in the hand of God, and He turns them wherever He pleases, just like the rivers of water.*

I, therefore, declare that men and women are working for my good, spiritually, physically, and in all circumstances.

I have favor with men and women, kings and princes, in all places.

Everything and every person is working for my own good henceforth, in Jesus name.

7. I Can Do All Things Through Christ

"I can do all this through him who gives me strength." - Philippians 4:13

DECLARE: *I have the life of God in me. I have His wisdom and strength working on the inside of me.*

Therefore I can do all things through Christ who supports me.

I have understanding, strength, and divine direction.

I am not a confused fellow overwhelmed with life and circumstances.

I am in complete control of my life and everything that comes my way, for the Holy Spirit, my Senior Partner, will always guide me on what to do and how to proceed.

By the Holy Spirit, I will always know what to do, when to do it and how to do it, at all times and in all circumstances.

In Jesus name.

Day 21: **God is Answering Your Prayers**

This is the confidence which we have before Him: that if we ask anything according to His will, He hears us.

And if we know that He hears and listens to us in whatever we ask, we have the assurance that He will grant our requests. – 1 John 5:14-15 (Paraphrased)

As humans, we sometimes wonder if the prayers we have said, declared and made will be answered. Today, be assured that *your prayers, made according to God's Words, are being answered.*

Don't judge your prayers based on how you feel. Our prayers are not answered based on our feelings. The Scripture above says once we have prayed according to God's will, that is according to the WORD OF GOD, that we have answers to our prayers.

That means all the prayers and declarations we have taken from the scriptures and declared are getting answered.

So what should we do next?

We should have that consciousness and be praiseful to God for answering our prayers.

We should be confident that this year will indeed be for us a year to arise and shine. Feelings have nothing to do with how God answers prayers. All prayers made according to God's WORDS are answered.

WHAT NEXT?

In the last couple of days, you have made several prayers, confessions, declarations, and supplications. God says that He will do exactly as you have spoken in His ears. Your prayers will be answered.

This year will be a year of all-round victory and total restoration. You will arise and shine this year. It will be a year of manifestation and testimonies.

Today, spend time thanking God for every prayer you have said and every declaration you have made. Speak into the spirit realm and seal your prayers with the Blood of Jesus Christ, and then minister to yourself; anoint yourself, your environment, and your family with oil, claiming healing, restoration, victory and ***divine breakthrough***...in Jesus name.

You can make the following prayers and declarations at any time. That means you can memorize any or all of them and declare them all through the day. But it is also highly recommended that you make out time and make these prayers.

FOR MEDITATION

Mark 11:24 - Therefore I say unto you, what things soever ye desire, when ye pray, believe that ye receive them, and ye shall have them.

1 John 5:14-15 - And this is the confidence that we have in him, that, if we ask anything according to his will, he hears us.

John 15:7 - If ye abide in me, and my words abide in you, ye shall ask what ye will, and it shall be done unto you.

Matthew 7:7 - Ask, and it shall be given you; seek, and ye shall find; knock, and it shall be opened unto you:

Jeremiah 33:3 - Call unto me, and I will answer thee, and shew thee great and mighty things, which thou knowest not.

1 John 3:22 - And whatsoever we ask, we receive of him, because we keep his commandments, and do those things that are pleasing in his sight.

Jeremiah 29:12 - Then shall ye call upon me, and ye shall go and pray unto me, and I will hearken unto you.

Hebrews 11:1 - Now faith is the substance of things hoped for, the evidence of things not seen.

PRAYERS AND DECLARATIONS

Heavenly Father, I have called on You in these past days. I have offered many prayers and declarations and supplications. I am here today to declare that I believe, according to Thy Word, that You have answered my prayers.

Father, I asked You for the forgiveness of my sins and the healing of my land, and according to Your Word. I declare that I believe that my sins have been forgiven, and my lands have been healed.

O Lord, I prayed that strongholds causing barriers between me and Your blessings be removed, and I thank You today because every stronghold in my life has been rolled away.

My family and I are no longer under any generational curse from this day forward because the curses have now been neutralized by the Blood of Jesus Christ, in Jesus name.

Monitoring demons over my life have been defeated, bound, and are now resting in the abyss until Jesus comes. I am now monitored and followed by the angels of God, who are working to bring to pass God's plans for   my   life.

From today, I have the spirit of boldness, love, power, and a sound mind. Fear is defeated in my life forever and ever. I will take bold steps ordained by God to bring me into my place of testimony from now onwards, in Jesus name.

The powers of witchcraft over my life, family, business, career, destiny, and environment have been destroyed, and they will remain destroyed forever and ever.

From this day on, I am taking back hundred-fold whatever has been damaged in my life and destiny due to witchcraft, in Jesus name

---

Father LORD, thank You for my deliverance from marine spirits and their operations. And thank You for making me seated in the heavenly places with Christ Jesus, far above principalities and powers and above the works of darkness, in Jesus name.

Today Lord, I remind You that I have prayed and reversed all manner of curses against my life, family, and destiny, and I want to tell You that I believe that no curse is working against me anymore, for whatever You do is permanent, in Jesus name.

I have victory over territorial demons, and through Jesus, their operations against my life, my family, and the Church of Jesus Christ have been defeated.

Lord, in this neighborhood, there will be a revival, and Your people shall have their prayers answered every day, to Your glory, in Jesus name.

I am free from any form of negative soul tie and oppression coming from evil men posing as men and women of God, in Jesus name.

I declare that afflictions and infirmity are defeated in my life and family, and my loved ones whom I have prayed for. The healing power of God is at work in my life and that of my loved ones from this day forward, in Jesus name.

Lord, I declare that my marriage and home is blessed.

I declare that we are enjoying financial abundance and divine favor every day, in Jesus name.

I am God's sheep. I hear His voice, and I follow Him. So I have direction and I make the right decisions from today onwards, in Jesus name.

Holy Spirit, I thank You for empowering me to produce all Your fruits in my life, and I thank You for Your gifts working through my life to bless my generation, in Jesus name.

O Lord, I take the full recovery of all my stolen blessings in the past. This year, my family and I are having total victory over the devil and his works. We have full restoration in every area of our lives, in Jesus name.

This year, I will arise and shine for my light is come. Even if darkness and gross darkness covers the earth, God's glory will be seen in my life, every day, every week, every month, and in every place I go, in Jesus name.

ANOINT YOURSELF AND YOUR ENVIRONMENT

Heavenly Father, I anoint myself today, my house, and this environment, and completely surrender and dedicate all to You.

I declare that my life, my family, and this place shall be holy unto You.

Just as Jesus was anointed with Holy Ghost and with power and He went about doing good and healing all who were oppressed by the devil, I also pray that my life, my family and this house and environment shall be a source from which good news, healing, encouragement, light, and favor shall flow through to others, in Jesus name.

THANK YOU, LORD, FOR DOING UNTO ME AS YOU HAVE HEARD ME SPEAK INTO YOUR EARS.

OFFER PRAISE UNTO GOD

Remember that today is the 21st day of your New Year prayer retreat. So, in addition to our prayers and declarations, it's a day to praise God in your own way. Bring God an offering of praise and worship. Sing and dance before Him, for He has given you victory. Do it anyhow you want. Play great music and worship God. Sing and make praise declarations.

DECLARATIONS OF PRAISE

Praise the Lord, my soul; all my inmost being, praise his holy name.

Praise the Lord, my soul, and forget not all his benefits, who forgives all your sins and heals all your diseases,

Who redeems your life from the pit and crowns you with love and compassion,

Who satisfies your desires with good things so that your youth is renewed like the eagle - **Psalm 103:1-5.**

You are the Lord God Almighty. Your praise and glory fill the earth. Your praise fills my life.

I thank you, Lord, with all my heart; I sing praise to You before the gods. I face your holy Temple, bow down, and praise your name because of Your constant love and faithfulness, because You have shown that Your name and your commands are supreme.

You answered me when I called to You; with Your strength, you strengthened me.

O Lord, even though you are so high above, You care for the lowly, and the proud cannot hide from you

You will do everything you have promised.

Lord, Your love is eternal. You will complete the work that you have begun **(Psalm 138:6-8)**

God

Bless

You

Get in Touch

We love testimonies. We love to hear what God is doing around the world as people draw close to Him in prayer.

So please share your story with us.

Also, please consider giving this book a review on Amazon and checking out our other titles at www.amazon.com/author/danielokpara.

I also invite you to check out our website at www.BetterLifeWorld.org and consider joining our newsletter, which we send out once in a while with great tips, testimonies, and revelations from God's Word for victorious living.

Feel free to drop us your prayer request. We will join faith with you, and God's power will be released into your life for your deliverance and testimony.

About the Author

Daniel Chika Okpara is an influential voice in contemporary Christian ministry. His mandate is to make lives better through the teaching and preaching of God's Word with signs and wonders. He is the resident pastor of Shining Light Christian Centre, a fast-growing church in the city of Lagos.

He is also the president and CEO of Better Life World Outreach Center, a non-denominational ministry dedicated to global evangelism, prayer revival and empowering of God's people with the WORD to make their lives better. Through his Breakthrough Prayers Foundation (www.breakthroughprayers.org), an online portal leading people all over the world to encounter God and change their lives through prayer, thousands of people encounter God through prayer, and hundreds of testimonies are received from all around the world.

As a foremost Christian teacher and author, his books are in high demand in prayer groups, Bible studies, and for personal devotions. He has authored over 50 life-transforming books and manuals on business, prayer, relationship, and victorious living, many of which have become international best-sellers.

He is a Computer Engineer by training and holds a Master's Degree in Christian Education from Continental Christian University. He is married to Doris Okpara, his best friend, and the most significant support in his life. They are blessed with lovely children.

WEBSITE: www.betterlifeworld.org

Other Books by the Same Author

1. Prayer Retreat: 21 Days Devotional With Over 500 Prayers & Declarations to Destroy Stubborn Demonic Problems.

2. HEALING PRAYERS & CONFESSIONS

3. 200 Violent Prayers for Deliverance, Healing, and Financial Breakthrough.

4. Hearing God's Voice in Painful Moments

5. Healing Prayers: Prophetic Prayers that Brings Healing

6. Healing WORDS: Daily Confessions & Declarations to Activate Your Healing.

7. Prayers That Break Curses and Spells and Release Favors and Breakthroughs.

8. 120 Powerful Night Prayers That Will Change Your Life Forever.

9. How to Pray for Your Children Everyday

10. How to Pray for Your Family

11. Daily Prayer Guide

12. Make Him Respect You: 31 Very Important Relationship Intelligence for Women to Make their Men Respect them.

13. How to Cast Out Demons from Your Home, Office & Property

14. Praying Through the Book of Psalms

15. The Students' Prayer Book

16. How to Pray and Receive Financial Miracle

17. Powerful Prayers to Destroy Witchcraft Attacks.

18. Deliverance from Marine Spirits

19. Deliverance From Python Spirit

20. Anger Management God's Way

21. How God Speaks to You

22. Deliverance of the Mind

23. 20 Commonly Asked Questions About Demons

24. Praying the Promises of God

25. When God Is Silent! What to Do When Prayer Seems Unanswered or Delayed

26. I SHALL NOT DIE: Prayers to Overcome the Spirit and Fear of Death.

27. Praise Warfare

28. Prayers to Find a Godly Spouse

29. How to Exercise Authority Over Sickness

30. Under His Shadow: Praying the Promises of God for Protection (Book 2).

NOTES

Made in the USA
Monee, IL
19 December 2019